Henry Norman

The Real Japan

Studies of Contemporary Japanese Manners, Morals, Administration, and Politics

Henry Norman

The Real Japan
Studies of Contemporary Japanese Manners, Morals, Administration, and Politics

ISBN/EAN: 9783337077785

Printed in Europe, USA, Canada, Australia, Japan

Cover: Foto ©Suzi / pixelio.de

More available books at **www.hansebooks.com**

THE REAL JAPAN.

"*Deus inde ego.*"—HORACE, *Sat.* 1., 8.

THE REAL JAPAN

STUDIES OF CONTEMPORARY JAPANESE MANNERS, MORALS, ADMINISTRATION, AND POLITICS

BY HENRY NORMAN

ILLUSTRATED FROM PHOTOGRAPHS BY THE AUTHOR

"*Hana yori dango*"

LONDON: T. FISHER UNWIN,
PATERNOSTER SQUARE. MDCCCXCII

" She came to me when Spring was in the land,—
    I could not separate her from its flowers;
    She was inwoven with the budding hours
    When summer's dainty leafery is planned.
    We stood a day or two on friendship's strand,
    As rightly met as April sun and showers;
    She came to me when Spring was in the land,—
    I could not separate her from its flowers."

PREFACE.

THE accessible works on Japan may be divided into two classes—large and elaborate treatises upon the history, geography, monuments, &c., of the country; and superficial narratives, often very entertaining, of the personal views and experiences of almost every literary wayfarer who has crossed the Pacific. The works of Rein are examples of the former class; every subscriber to a circulating library could mention a dozen of the latter.

No writer has yet given an account of the political, economic, educational, and social conditions resulting from the present era of so-called " Enlightened Peace." Indeed, the progress of the Japanese people has been so rapid toward civilization as the word is understood by Western nations, and the crystallization of this into actual institutions is still proceeding so actively, that it is doubtful whether such a work is yet possible. Before the author could return his proof-sheets to the *printer, the institutions he was describing* would often have undergone *a vital modification.*

The present essays constitute an attempt, faute de mieux, *to place before the readers of the countries whence Japan is deriving her incentives and her ideas an account of some of the chief aspects and institutions of Japanese life as it really is to-day. Nothing is claimed for these essays beyond honesty of intention, and such accuracy as personal pains and unusual opportunities can afford. My statements are based upon months of special investigation at the capital, supplemented by visits for the same purpose to Siberia, Korea, and Peking. At Tōkyō every opportunity for study of all the departments of Government was most courteously afforded me; a Japanese gentleman from the Civil Service was placed at my disposal as translator and interpreter; and my inquiries into matters outside Government control were made easy by official and private assistance.*

For these facilities I have to express my great thanks in equal measure to H. E. Count Ito, H. E. Count Inouye, *and* H. E. Viscount Aoki. *To Mr.* H. W. Denison, *of the Japanese Foreign Office, I am indebted for much information and kind assistance from his intimate acquaintance with Japanese affairs. Most of all, however, I am under obligations to my friend*

PREFACE.

Captain F. Brinkley, R.A., the editor and proprietor of the Japan Mail—obligations I have tried to acknowledge elsewhere.

A number of these essays have appeared at different times in newspaper form in England (in the Pall Mall Gazette and several other journals), the United States, and France. Several are new, and all have been revised and extended. With the exception of three negatives kindly placed at my service by Professor W. K. Burton, of the Japanese Imperial University, almost all the illustrations are from photographs taken by myself. I have to thank Mr. Joseph Pennell and Mr. George Thomson for kind and accomplished help in making a number of them more suitable for mechanical reproduction.

H. N.

ADEN, October 19, 1891.

CONTENTS.

I.
AT HOME IN JAPAN 17

II.
JAPANESE JOURNALISM 35

III.
JAPANESE JUSTICE 59

IV.
JAPANESE EDUCATION 87

V.
JAPAN AS AN EASTERN POWER 107

VI.
ARTS AND CRAFTS IN JAPAN:—I. AMONG THE TÔKYÔ ARTIFICERS 135

VII.
ARTS AND CRAFTS IN JAPAN:—II. PAST AND PRESENT . 153

VIII.
JAPANESE WOMEN 175

IX.

	PAGE
JAPANESE JINKS	201

X.

IN RURAL JAPAN: A RUSH TO A VOLCANO . . . 237

XI.

THE YOSHIWARA: AN UNWRITTEN CHAPTER OF JAPANESE LIFE 275

XII.

JAPAN FOR THE JAPANESE? 307

XIII.

THE FUTURE OF JAPAN 335

LIST OF ILLUSTRATIONS.

	PAGE
"DEUS INDE EGO"	*Frontispiece*
AT HOME IN JAPAN	21
IN MR. MORIOKA'S GARDEN	25
"GOOD AFTERNOON!"	29
A *GEISHA* DANCING—I.	39
CAPTAIN BRINKLEY, R.A.	54
A JAPANESE POLICEMAN	62
A *GEISHA* DANCING—II.	73
ON THE CONVICT FARM	77
THE PRISON RICE-MILL	81
WAITING FOR THE CONDEMNED	85
AN OLD WARRIOR	109
A *GEISHA* DANCING—III.	119
JAPANESE ARTILLERY.—"FIRE!"	129
THE IVORY-CARVER'S STUDIO	142
A *GEISHA* DANCING—IV	165
EN DESHABILLE	181
AFTER THE BATH	194

LIST OF ILLUSTRATIONS.

	PAGE
"THE LATEST STYLE"	197
A GEISHA DANCING—V.	205
"SHE HAS RETIRED"	221
"MISS FATE"	227
A TUNE ON THE MOON-FIDDLE	230
A CLASSIC DANCE	241
OUR RUNNERS AT THE WELL	247
AT THE EDGE OF THE PRECIPICE	260
AFTER THE EARTHQUAKE	265
A FAN DANCE	269
A KASHI-ZASHIKI	281
A PROCESSIONIST OF YOSHIWARA	287
THE YUJO	292
THE VISIT TO THE FLOWERS OF YOSHIWARA	299
HACHIMONJI-NI-ARUKU	303
A MATSURI IN YOKOHAMA	342
ONE ASPECT OF "THE REAL JAPAN"	349

ALSO, ILLUSTRATIONS ON PP. 19, 34, 37, 89, 106, 137, 144, 152, 155, 177, 191, 199, 203, 208, 236, 239, 274, 277, 306, 337, 365.

I.
AT HOME IN JAPAN.

I.

AT HOME IN JAPAN.

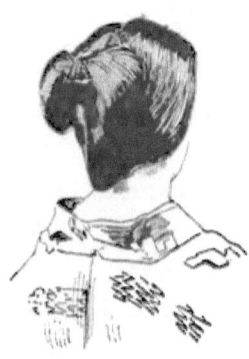

THE Japanese house is the offspring of the earthquake. It is light and flat, and never more than two-storeyed. High and heavy buildings are always in danger in Japan. Professor Milne has invented an earthquake-thwarting method, namely, to interpose a handful of large round shot between the corner posts and the foundations, thus providing for free oscillation. This method may be admirably adapted to cure a real earthquake, but it has the effect of creating a succession of imaginary ones, and the "earthquake thrill" is too precious an emotion to be vulgarized by such mechanical limitation. Fujisan does not, indeed, "buck like a mustang" here, as the Arkansaw man said his mountain did, when the earth trembles, but everybody has run for his life once or twice, and several people have been surprised to see their chimney introducing itself into their bed, plunging them into the state of mind of the Irishman who exclaimed, when his excited horse caught its hind foot in the stirrup, "If you're goin' to git on, I'm goin' to git off!" The ceiling in the billiard room of the Tōkyō Club is bolted to the walls by a network of iron bars and ties, stretching overhead like the web an antediluvian spider might have stretched to catch an ichtheosaurus. "What on earth is all that for?" asked an astonished visitor. "If you had seen the cues hopping about and the balls flying, and the tables doing a double shuffle round the room two months ago, while the members themselves disappeared like rabbits through the windows, you wouldn't ask," was the reply. Yet since "Earthquake Milne" has set traps for the rumbler (he calls them "Seismographs") the earthquakes seem to be migrating. But a little one caught us once while I was interviewing a Minister of State, and rattled the chandelier overhead in a manner that caused us to draw back simultaneously to see if we had not dropped a handkerchief under the chair, and stopped a Japanese sentence in the middle—a feat which nothing less than an earthquake could accomplish. It was of no use for the private

AT HOME IN JAPAN.

secretary to look at the door and say "Come in!" I knew in an instant what it was.

But how to describe a Japanese house, where nothing is like anything corresponding to it at home? The address—Kojimachiku, Ichibancho, Sijiuniban—does not throw much light on it. From the outside it is an uninviting big black barn; inside it is a spotless doll's house magnified a thousand diameters, all wood and wicker and white paper. The entrance hall is a platform raised a couple of feet above the ground, where you take off your boots if you are a foreigner, or leave your sandals if you are Japanese. A screen door slides back and you are in—but that depends upon circumstances. Sometimes you are in one room and sometimes in another. It may be a general sitting-room fifty feet square; it may be a bedroom (if you call early in the morning); or you may find yourself in an improvised sanctum and intruding upon somebody writing laboured descriptions for a far-away public. For here walls have not only ears, they have also legs, and when you wish to make a new room you simply "form square" by sliding enough panels in their grooves to enclose the space, or at your pleasure all the rooms can be thrown into one, enclosed, in our case, by forty-six panels. Those forming the sides of the house consist each of sixty little paper panes. To wet one's finger, stick it silently into the window and peep through, is thus the natural Japanese counterpart of Occidental surreptitious inspection by the keyhole. The floor is of mats; not mats strewed about as at home, but solid structures of delicate stuffed wicker, an inch thick, of conventional and regular size, let into the floor,—elastic, spotless, immovable, never profaned by even the daintiest of slippers. Chairs and tables are, of course, unknown, and the posture of repose is to seat oneself on one's heels. This squatting, by the way, is very painful at first, and like the "blameless dances" in 'Ruddigore," "takes a deal of training." At meal times you squat anywhere and your food is placed before you. When you are tired you throw yourself anywhere on the floor, with no fear of spoiling your white linen suit. When evening comes you do not seek your bed chamber, you simply make it, by sliding the walls round the spot you have chosen for your slumbers. The rough and ready way is to tread around on the floor till you find a specially soft mat, and then lay a few walls upon it for a couch. A more luxurious one is to have a *futon* or thick quilt spread out, and roll yourself in a rug or blanket upon it. The chief drawback for a foreigner is that his hip-bone, which is much more prominent than that of a Japanese, is terribly in the way if he has not learned the traveller's trick of obliterating the natural projections of the body.

But you sleep comfortably in spite of the marauding rat, whose immunity from attack has rendered him equally inquisitive and harmless, and in the morning when you return from the bath, bed and bedroom have alike disappeared. It is the story of Aladdin domesticated.

The bath, again, is a new experience. Take an enormous oval bucket, holding perhaps fifty gallons, with a stove-pipe running up inside it. Fill the tub with water and the pipe with red-hot charcoal, and when the temperature is a little short of boiling point, get bodily in and sit down, and you have a Japanese bath. In most cases the next step is to get out again with amazing alacrity, but the Japanese sits calmly there and perspires till he is parboiled. Being the guest, I am invited to enter first, while the entire household stands round and suppresses its amusement. When I emerge, in a fainting condition, my host enters, and he is followed in turn by the five servants in the order of their dignity, down to the humble "cook-boy." If there were any ladies resident in our household they would take their turn with the rest. This bath is, of course, merely to open the pores. One is not supposed to wash in it, but to sit quite still.

In Mr. Morioka's Garden.

Soaping follows for the foreigners and rubbing for the others, and the cold douche. The process when completed is delicious, cleansing, and invigorating, and far ahead of the simple "cold tub" of the Englishman at home and abroad.

Behind every Japanese house, however small or humble, there is a garden, though it is given to few to have one like that here shown, Mr. Morioka's at Honjo, where I received such never-to-be-forgotten hospitality. In ours, there are the huge-leaved palms, the pleasant shady maples, the amusing bamboo, and a host of shrubs with odd and gaudy blossoms. Colossal bumble-bees go rumbling round; there is always a pair of brilliant broad-winged butterflies dancing together; and every now and then one of the great half-tame scavenging crows, of which there are hundreds of thousands not only tolerated but protected in Japan, puts his coal-black head right into the room where we are sitting and salutes us with his hoarse and comical "Ah!" But the bamboo is the funniest. One morning we discern a tiny pointed green shoot in the grass. By evening it is well above the ground. In twenty-four hours it would make a respectable walking stick, and if you should be so ill-advised as to hang your hat on it at night you could not reach it next morning, and would have either to sacrifice the enterprising bamboo or to be satisfied to see your head-covering gradually disappear in the clouds.

When guests arrive, say for dinner, the politeness of paradise is turned loose. With great apparent hesitation they enter, bowing low with their hands on their knees if they are men, or dropping on their knees and touching their foreheads almost to the ground if they are ladies. The first Japanese salutation corresponds exactly to the Norwegian " Tak for sidst,"—" Thank you for the pleasure I had the last time I met you." This, however, is but the merest beginning of Japanese greeting. A conversation something after this style ensues :—

"I beg your pardon for my rudeness on the last occasion."

"How can you say such a thing when it was I who failed to show you due courtesy?"

"Far from it! I received a lesson in good manners from you."

" How can you condescend to come to such a poor house as this?"

"How can you, indeed, be so kind as to receive

such an unimportant person as myself under your distinguished roof?"

All this punctuated with low bows and the sound of breath sucked rapidly in between the teeth, expressive of great *empressement.* At last, amid a final chorus of *Arigato*, the guests come to anchor upon the floor. Various objects are

"GOOD AFTERNOON!"

handed to them to entertain them, a curio or two, a few photographs, anything, no matter what, for it is *de rigueur* in Japanese etiquette to affect a great interest and admiration on such occasions.

Then dinner begins (I am describing now, of course, the hospitality we receive, rather than that which it is in our power to extend) with the production of a lacquer tray on which is a small bowl of the same material filled with soup and fish—a species of *bouillabaisse*. Having drunk the soup out of the bowl, you eat the fish with your chop-sticks. It is an error, by the way, to suppose that it is difficult to acquire the use of this Oriental knife and fork. Nothing is easier. After the fish comes a lacquer dish with four or five little heaps of food on it—a *purée* of chestnuts, a *salmi* of some small bird or wild-fowl, a few boiled lily-roots, and a mess of stewed seaweed. With the chop-sticks a small portion of each of these is lifted in epicurean alternation. Now *saké* is produced in a porcelain or silver bottle, with a bowl of water and a number of tiny cups, each holding a tablespoonful. *Saké* resembles dry sherry, and is always served warm. You never help yourselves to *saké*, but the servants—usually girls—squatting in an outer ring round the diners (everybody being, of course, on mats on the floor) take care that your cup is always full. The Japanese version of " A glass of wine with you, sir," is peculiar. You empty your cup, plunge it into the bowl of clean water, move off your mat, and after touching the cup to your forehead, offer it upon your open palm, and with a low bow to the person you desire to toast. He receives it in the same manner, with an expression of appreciation, and the servant immediately fills it for him. A few minutes afterwards he returns it with similar ceremony. With the actual drinking there is no sentiment whatever in Japan—no "Good health!" as with us, no "A la vôtre!" no "Prosit!" no "Skaal!"—the ceremony begins and ends with the passing of the cup. Nor is there any of the valour of those who "gloried and drank deep;" you drink often in Japan; it is impossible to drink deep in an inch of liquor. With the valour, disappear, too, all such legends and poetry as have clustered about King Olaf's drinking-horn and the Teutonic "Becher" and the more gentle Anglo-Saxon "Loving Cup." And finally, the teetotaler may not set a gain in sobriety over against the loss in valour and in verse. It is just as easy to get tipsy out of a teaspoon as out of a flagon, and much more humiliating. In fact, drinking as an heroic exercise is not without its votaries in Japan. I have just read in a Japanese newspaper that in Kyoto last year a number of confirmed topers formed themselves into a society which they styled "The Kyoto Sakenomi Kai" (*Saké-*

drinkers' Association.) One of the rules states that an absolutely essential qualification for membership is the ability to consume at least three *sho* of *saké* at a sitting, and this test has been most conscientiously fulfilled by the twenty-three members. A resident of Kyoto applied for admission the other day, and proved himself worthy of a high place among the brotherhood by drinking eight *sho* of *saké* (sufficient to fill about twenty quart bottles) during the initiation ceremonies. There is talk of electing him president of the society.

So far the Japanese dinner is excellent. At the next course, however, most foreigners cry halt. Upon a tiny wire gridiron appear several pink and white morsels, accompanied by various Lilliputian salads and a good-looking sauce. These are raw fish, exquisite in appearance but execrable in the mouth. After them come cakes of many kinds, and tea, and finally, when you wish to retire you give the signal by asking for rice. I should have said that the "tobacco bon," a box containing a small brazier, a Japanese pipe, and a section of bamboo serving the unpleasantly conspicuous purpose of combined ash-receptacle and spittoon, is brought in at an early stage, and even when ladies are present you can smoke as many pipes of the mild and aromatic Japanese tobacco, each consisting of two whiffs, as you please. The feast is prolonged by ceaseless conversation, a thousand jests at which everybody roars with laughter, and an endless series of mutual compliments. Delicate in form and in substance, characterized by infinite kindliness and merriment, subject to strict and immemorial rules, a Japanese dinner is typical of the Japanese people. Most foreigners are delighted with it as a novel experience, and hasten to supplement it with a beefsteak or a dish of poached eggs.

One invariable accompaniment to such an entertainment I have purposely omitted to mention—the *geisha*, or girl-musicians, who appear during dinner and dance to the *samisen* and the *biwa* and *ni-gen-king*. Tiny creatures of fairyland they are, so exquisitely dressed, so wonderfully *coiffées*, so pretty and graceful and clever and full of fun, true visitors from Oriental wonderland. These and their like demand at least a chapter to themselves.

Dinner brings the Japanese day to a close. The guests rise from their mats, and steal away, not silently by any means, and as ceremoniously as they entered. When the last pair of sandals has been resumed, and the last *jinrikisha* has whirled away, our servants slide the heavy shutters into their places all round the house, in a trice bedrooms and beds appear, and from the waking dream of being "At Home in Japan" one passes by an easy transition into that land of other dreams where alone every wanderer is in truth at home, however many thousand leagues of sea and land divide him from what he loves.

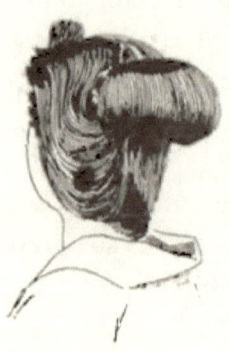

II.

JAPANESE JOURNALISM.

II.

JAPANESE JOURNALISM.

THE watch-dogs of civilization sleep with one eye open in Japan, as well as in Fleet Street or Broadway, and it is fast becoming true that "there's not a place where man may dwell," but the interviewer dwells there too. Four interviewers for the vernacular press called upon me before I had been forty-eight hours on Japanese soil, and when I succumbed, after vainly pleading privilege, it was to find that the alert-minded Japanese has simply taken the American system of interviewing and reduced it to its simplest terms, not to say *ad absurdum*. With him interviewing is strict business from the start, like pulling a tooth or boring a hole, and he wastes no time like his trans-Pacific archetype over pleasant introductory remarks about the weather or your voyage. The operation is as follows. You receive a card bearing a series of cabalistic marks, and, uncertain whether your visitor is a Minister of State or a guide in want of a job, you go downstairs and discover a dapper little gentleman, in appearance about nineteen, dressed in faultless foreign fashion, tennis-shoes, flannel trousers, white waistcoat, blue coat, flowing necktie, spectacles and pith-helmet, and speaking English with the accuracy and impressiveness of a copy-book. "Good morning. Are you Mr. Blank?" "Good morning. I am." "I am the reporter of the *So-and-so* newspaper of Tōkyō. Will you permit me to interview you?" "With pleasure." The interviewer then takes a seat, produces a note-book and pencil, and begins with the directness of a census-taker. "How old are you, and where were you born?" And when I tell him that I was "born of poor but respectable parents" in the year one, let us say, he gravely commits the unfamiliar phrase to paper. "How long will you stay?—how long since you started?—where have you been?—how do you like Japan?—what do they think of Japan in

A *Geisha* Dancing.—I.

(*An Instantaneous Photograph.*)

England?—what is it expected will become of Korea?—will there be war between England and Russia?—will Ireland get Home Rule?"—these were all among the questions he pressed upon me with the relentless persistence of a pile-driver. At last, when I had been compelled to draw liberally upon my imagination for my facts, and the note-book of the enemy of travelling mankind was full, I supposed that the interview was over. Nothing could have been further from the interviewer's idea. He settled himself in his chair, re-sharpened his pencil, produced a new note-book, and said, "If anything of interest has ever befallen you upon your travels, please give me full informations now." This was too much, and when I said to him as he was going, "If you do me the favour of sending me a copy of the *So-and-so* containing this interview, will you be kind enough to put a mark upon it so that I may know which is the right way upwards," I thought a twinkle in his eye showed it was dawning upon him at last that to cross-question a solitary and ill-informed individual upon the policies of all nations and the details of his own obscure life, was really a huge joke. But I had my doubts again afterwards when, sure enough, I received an extraordinary looking newspaper with "top" solemnly written on one side of it.

Japanese interviewing, however, like interviewing elsewhere, frequently renders a service to the community, for ministers of state, even, and many less important personages, are not averse to making their views known on occasion in this way. But journalism has come with a rush in Japan, and there are at the present time too many newspapers for any one of them to have the circulation and therefore the means to become as influential and as enterprising as the great journals of Europe and America. In the whole of Japan there are no fewer than 550 newspapers and periodicals, and in the capital of Tōkyō alone there are seventeen political dailies, with a combined monthly circulation of 3,906,000, and 116 periodicals, circulating together 495,000 copies. With such competition, circulations are of course very small, the largest in Tōkyō, whichever newspaper has it, being probably not much over 10,000 copies, half of them sold in the city itself, and half in the villages around and other towns.[1]

[1] An official statistician gives 95,932,270 as the number of copies of "Journaux et diverses brochures publiées" in the whole of Japan during 1887.

A Japanese newspaper is a very different thing from what we are accustomed to find on our breakfast tables. Our last page is its first; its columns only run half the length of the page; it has no such thing as head lines or "scare heads," and its titles run from top to bottom instead of across; it has but a few rough illustrations; it prints few advertisements, but those are paid for at a comparatively high rate; its price is low, ranging from one to two cents a copy and from 25 to 50 cents a month; and it knows nothing yet of sensational advertisements, or flaming posters, or deeds of journalistic "derring do." In general, its scale is much more that of the French newspaper than the world-moving monsters of London and New York. The only evidence of it that one sees in the streets is the newsman, either a lank and lean middle-aged man or else a boy, clad in meagre cotton clothes, trotting along with a bundle of neatly folded papers under his arm and announcing his passage by the incessant tinkling of a little brass bell tied to his waistband behind.

The internal organization of a newspaper office is a sad spectacle of daily struggle with difficulties unknown elsewhere and really unnecessary here.

The Japanese written and printed character consists of the Chinese ideographs, those complicated square figures made up of an apparent jumble of zig-zags and crosses and ticks and triangles and tails—"the footprints of a drunken fly"—and of the original Japanese syllabary, called *kana*. Of the former there are 20,000 in all, of which perhaps 14,000 constitute the scholars' vocabulary, and no fewer than 4,000 are in common daily use; while the forty-seven simple character of *kana* are known to everybody.[1] Therefore the Japanese compositor has to be prepared to place in his stick any one of over 4,000 different types—truly an appalling task. From the nature of the problem several consequences naturally follow. First, he must be a good deal of a scholar himself, to recognize all these instantly and accurately; secondly, his eye-sight suffers fearfully, and he generally wears a huge pair of magnifying goggles; and third, as it is physically impossible for any one man to

---

[1] As an example of the combined intricacy and formality of the Japanese language, a Tōkyō newspaper recently calculated that in the Department of Justice alone seventy-five working days were consumed annually in writing one honorific prefix in official correspondence. This prefix has now been abolished except in letters addressed to the Court.

reach 4,000 types, a totally different method of case arrangement has to be devised. The "typo," therefore, of whom there are only three or four on a paper, sits at a little table at one end of a large room, with the case containing his forty-seven *kana* syllables before him. From end to end of the room tall cases of type are arranged like the shelves in a crowded library, a passage three feet wide being left between each two. The compositor receives his "copy" in large pieces, which he cuts into little "takes," and hands each of these to one of half a dozen boys who assist him. The boy takes this and proceeds to walk about among the cases till he has collected each of the ideographs, or square Chinese picture-words, omitting all the *kana* syllables which connect them. While these boys are thus running to and fro, snatching up the types and jostling each other, they keep up a continual chant, singing the name of the character they are looking for, as they cannot recognize it till they hear its sound, the ordinary lower-class Japanese not understanding his daily paper unless he reads it aloud. When a boy has collected all the square characters of his "take," he lays them upon it by the side of the compositor, who sets them up in proper order in his composing-stick, adding the connecting *kana* from the case before him. Then a proof is pulled, as with us, and taken to two proof-readers, one of whom sings the "copy" aloud to the other. A Japanese composing-room is thus a scene of bustle and noise and laughter and weird noises, the only serious figure being the long-haired "typo," seated afar off by himself and poring over his wretched spider-web letters like some old entomologist with a new beetle under his microscope. The "making up" and stereotyping is like that of old-fashioned offices at home, and the paper is printed upon flat presses fed by hand. The total number of persons employed on a typical Japanese newspaper, say the *Nichi Nichi Shimbun*, is as follows:—One political director, one chief editor, five assistant editors, four proof-readers, one shorthand-writer, twelve reporters or news gatherers, three or four compositors, each with several assistants, twelve men in the press-room, and minor *employés*, including distributors, making a total of 150 persons. The reporters are the weak point, for the editor frankly tells you that if they cannot find news they are compelled to bring home fiction, as they are paid by results, and even then they do not often earn more than £2 or $10 a month. They therefore deliberately invent a large part of their news. For example, a few months ago almost all the vernacular newspapers published long and circumstantial harrowing accounts of the eruption of Zoozan, a small mountain in the province of Bingo, and the foreign press copied them, the whole affair being a myth. During my own stay the vernacular press had fifty items of news about my movements, of ludicrous inaccuracy. So untrustworthy, indeed, is the reporter that an assistant editor is always sent when anybody of importance desires or is invited to be interviewed. A reporter of the *Tōkyō Shimpo* once actually listened outside the council chamber where the Cabinet met, and printed the broken sentences he overheard! As regards the supply of news, the best papers have their own correspondents, almost always men employed on a newspaper in other chief cities, and some of them have mail correspondents abroad, generally young men who have gone to Europe or America to study. Much enterprise is shown in collecting full accounts of anything that occurs in Japan, but the trail of the untrustworthy reporter is over it all, and this greatly reduces its interest and influence. Most of the papers are owned each by a few rich and influential men who keep in the background.

If this estimate of the Japanese press errs, it does so on the side of leniency. One of the most qualified observers of things Japanese has written :—" The verdict of any candid reader of Japanese journals is that they have not reached even the threshold of achievement. Their local correspondence is virtually non-existent. Their foreign correspondence is a matter of accident. They have no telegraphic service worthy of the name, a few scanty messages from the provinces, representing the whole duty done for them by an agent that now fills the most important place in the columns of all Western newspapers. Their reporting is almost a by-word. They do not even give their readers any accurate information about the cases tried in the Law Courts, and in the great majority of instances no reliance can be placed on the items of miscellaneous intelligence they unhesitatingly publish. Yet with these shortcomings staring them in the face, they have engaged in such a headlong competition, that a copy of one of the best among them costs only seven-fortieths of a penny."

The oldest Tōkyō newspaper, and perhaps the leading one in Japan, is the *Nichi Nichi Shimbun* —" Daily News"—of which Mr. N. Seki is editor and part proprietor. Mr. Seki is a typical Japanese gentleman of the type produced by the modern tendencies of his nation. Personally a young man of fine features and charming manners, he is at the same time a political student with well-reasoned convictions upon politics and political economy in the abstract, and very definite views, if perhaps too enthusiastic ones, as to the practical application of his theories to the problems and needs of his own time and people. Like almost all educated modern Japanese he speaks English with ease, and on his recent return from a European trip of political studies—spent chiefly in London—he turned over a new leaf in his newspaper. For years the *Nichi Nichi Shimbun* had been regarded as the mouthpiece of the Government, and the happy possessor of the advantages which spring from such a connection. Indeed one Government official, who ought to know, told me the exact amount in dollars of the subsidy it received. But on the whole, as Mr. Seki discovered, the disadvantages of such a connection heavily outweigh the advantages, and nowhere does the suspicion of official subsidy do more injury than in the Japanese press.

On a par with this paper, or close on its heels, comes the *Jiji Shimpo*—the "Times"—an independent radical journal. This, like so many in Paris, several in the United States, and at least one in London, is a one-man organ—the mouthpiece of one man with original and characteristic opinions, and independent even to "conscientious unscrupulousness" in expressing them. The *Jiji Shimpo* has therefore all the peculiar strength and weakness of this course. The man is Mr. Fukuzawa, one of the most interesting and remarkable personalities in Japan. He began by translating into Japanese all the best foreign manuals of history, political economy, geography, philosophy, &c., and thus directing the youth of Japan to the best paths of Western knowledge. He has been for many years the head of the largest private school in Japan, where his influence over 700 or 800 young men was formerly boundless. To great learning he unites the highest degree of personal magnetism and extraordinary eloquence, so that if he chooses to make himself prominent in politics during the next few years, when the introduction of representative government will have given to public speaking the same place and power that it has among Western nations, he will become a force for the professional politicians to reckon with. His temperament, however, is that of the dreamer rather than that of the actor or the practical guide, and under his rule the *Jiji Shimpo* is constantly putting forth great schemes of reform which strike the imagination without offering any point of contact with practical affairs. Once he proposed, for instance, that financial reform should be begun by cutting off one-half of the salaries of all Government officials, as though the poor stipends of the nations' clerks all put together would be more than a drop in the bucket of national expenditure. Then again he lost caste greatly even among his own students by his proposal that Christianity, in which he professed, in common, as he said, with all intelligent men, to feel no personal faith, should be universally adopted for political ends. The *Jiji Shimpo* is always thoughtful and suggestive, but its suggestions—or rather Mr. Fukuzawa's—are

Emersonian in their subtlety and incomprehensibility, and Carlylean in their vigour and inaccuracy.

Among the newspapers of the Capital the *Hochi Shimbun*—the "Post"—is second to none, and its position is due not a little to the fact that it has been distinctly the organ of H. E. Count Okuma, ex-Minister of Foreign Affairs, Mr. Yano, the editor, having been formerly closely associated with Count Okuma in active political life. The Japanese Ministers are well acquainted with all the tactics of Western Ministers, and Prince Bismarck knows no more about the press or its value or its dangers than Count Okuma does.

Among the other leading papers are the *Mainichi Shimbun* ("every day's news"), a liberal journal owned by Mr. Numa, the speaker of the Tōkyō Assembly, and edited by Mr. Shimada; the *Choya Shimbun* ("official and popular news"), a liberal paper edited by Mr. Yoshida; the *Tōkyō Dempo* ("Telegraph"), a conservative journal, generally regarded as the organ of General Tani, formerly Minister of Agriculture and Commerce; and the *Koron Shinipo* ("public opinion"), newly established like the preceding one, but a radical paper, the organ of Count Itagaki, a radical "Jingo," edited by a Japanese member of the English bar, now residing abroad for awhile under the recent Peace Preservation Acts. The *Koron Shimpo* is closely associated, too, with Count Goto, a politician of much activity of mind, although he has never yet succeeded in forming a steady nucleus of political principles around which to gather that radical and opposition party he is credited with the desire to lead. The terms "liberal" and "conservative" and "radical," however, as thus applied to Japanese politicians and the Japanese press, must necessarily be misleading or at any rate very vague, until the debates of the National Assembly naturally result in the formation of distinct parties. At present statesmen, and therefore newspapers as well, are divided according to their personal differences upon each question as it arises.

I come now to the leading English daily paper in this part of the East, the *Japan Mail*, although it would perhaps have been more in accordance with the position and influence of that paper if I had begun with it. As in the case of Mr. Fukuzawa and the *Jiji Shimpo*, so—with a great difference—the *Japan Mail* springs every day from the brains of one man. It is edited and owned by Captain F. Brinkley, R.A., who began life in the East in 1866 as *aide de camp* to his cousin, Sir Richard Graves Macdonnell, then Governor of Hongkong. In 1867 he came to Yokohama in command of the artillery stationed there, and two years later, with the permission of the Horse Guards, accepted the position of teacher of strategy and tactics to the troops of the Prince of Echizen, one of the greatest of the feudal Daimios. The Resstoration abolished forces of this kind, and Captain Brinkley then entered the service of the Mikado's Government and took charge of the School for Marine Officers. By and by the Marines were abolished in Japan, and then he became professor of mathematics in the Engineering College. When in the onward march of Japan she dispensed with all foreign

CAPTAIN BRINKLEY, R.A.

professors except technical ones, Captain Brinkley purchased the *Japan Mail*. This was in 1881, and he has transformed it from a local sheet to a journal ranking with any in the East, and the recognized authority upon Japanese affairs the world over. Captain Brinkley is truly a remarkable man, and though the loss to Japan would probably be irremediable, one cannot help regretting that his great ability should not find its natural scope in some Western capital. His knowledge of the Japanese language, certainly so far as it is spoken, is much beyond that of any other foreigner; its modern history, its politics, its finance, and its foreign relations, he knows on the whole, it is hardly too much to say, as well as any Japanese living; as an authority upon Chinese and Japanese porcelain and faience he has no equal, and his collections are famous among connoisseurs everywhere; he is on intimate personal terms with the Japanese ministers and the foreign representatives alike, and not alone during the stormy times of Treaty Revision, but also on many other occasions, his personal tact and the masterly editorials of the *Japan Mail* have played an important part in the fortunes and foreign relations of the Japanese Empire. Indeed, the editor of one of the vernacular papers I have described at length above, said to me once, "Captain Brinkley's knowledge of the Japanese is marvellous—he knows everything about us—everything!" Add to this that he is as jolly and kind-hearted an Irishman as ever sang, "Whack for the larrily" in Kerry, or upset a pitcher in Coleraine, and that his knowledge, his experience, his collections, and his time are put with unfailing patience at the service of everybody who is really and genuinely interested in the Empire where he has made his home, and it is hardly necessary for me to go on and say that I am under the greatest obligations to him—obligations altogether too great for detailed acknowledgment. It would surprise readers at home to know how large and exact a part of all that they have recently read on Japan has been the direct result of "picking Brinkley's brains." Let me, at least, be explicit on this point.

There are at Yokohama two other papers published in English, the *Herald* and the *Gazette*. They are, however, purely the organs of the local foreign commercial community, their creed is "foreigners, especially Englishmen, right or wrong," and they make little or no attempt to understand or to represent Japanese thought and feeling.

Finally, to return to the vernacular press for a moment, the same thing must happen before long in Japan that has happened nearly everywhere else. The right man will get hold of one of the old newspapers, he will secure the support of an enterprising capitalist, he will flood Japan with advertisements, he will employ all the aids of illustration, he will revive the national art of fiction, he will engage foreign correspondents everywhere, he will make reputations and ruin them, he will create ministries, and destroy them, he will do much more good and evil than any of his fellow men, and by and by he will fill the pockets of his proprietors with a golden harvest, and then break down from over-work and die forgotten, like most other great editors before him. But—*vogue la galère!*

III.

JAPANESE JUSTICE.

III.

JAPANESE JUSTICE.

A JAPANESE policeman was never known to smile, but when he finds it necessary to proceed to the extreme step of arresting a law-breaker his face becomes clouded over with a pall of sorrow and solemnity that would do credit to an Irish undertaker taking the coffin-measurement of an archbishop. Grasping the offender firmly with one hand, with the other he extracts from an invisible pocket of great capacity a roll of strong cord. Whispering polite and minute directions in the ear of the victim, who obeys them with scrupulous consideration for the feelings of his captor, he winds the cord several times round his waist and then attaches his wrists in optical contact with the small of his back. Six feet of cord remain, the policeman grasps the loose end, and bowing to the prisoner with an "After you, Sir," the pair march away in a touching union of sadness and security. The neighbourhood is paralyzed during the performance, business is suspended, traffic is stopped, and the bob-tailed top-knot of *Bo-chan* the baby stands straight up from his cranium in alarm and disapprobation. But the moment the polite policeman and his politer prey have disappeared round the corner, all the spectators burst out laughing simultaneously, and two minutes afterwards the affair is forgotten by everybody except baby *Bo-chan's* brother, who inaugurates a series of abortive attempts to tie up the astonished and indignant cat, quite oblivious of the fact that the spider-and-fly manœuvre he has just witnessed requires for its successful accomplishment the coöperation of both parties. "Why on earth doesn't the

A JAPANESE POLICEMAN.

Japanese policeman use handcuffs?" I give it up.

The formality of an arrest, however, is the only amusing side of Japanese justice. If you follow the white-clothed policeman and his prisoner you will soon reach a police-station in which sit a dozen clerks and functionaries hard at work at books and accounts and reports, with nothing except their physiognomy and the little teapot and tobacco brazier beside each one to differentiate them from similar European officials. The prisoner will be taken before a superior officer, the charge against him noted down, he will be searched and then put in one of a dozen wooden cells, ten feet square perhaps, separated from the central passage by great wooden bars reaching from floor to ceiling, and making a cell curiously like an elephant house, but providing admirably for ventilation in a hot climate. At the police-station he may not be kept more than twenty-four hours, and then he is removed to a central station which is simply the first police-station on a large scale, minus the functionaries and plus the necessary arrangements for the detention of prisoners for long periods.

It is when the time for his regular trial comes

that the English or American investigator who has been following the offender's career finds himself on unfamiliar ground. But the unfamiliarity of it is far from being Japanese or Oriental, and to a Frenchman it would be home, sweet home. For the eclecticism of Japan, in proving all our western institutions and holding fast to those which seem to her good, results here at the centre of government in what looks like an international hodge-podge, until one has learned to appreciate the national principle which has produced it. Thus when you visit one of the purely political offices, say the Foreign Office, you find yourself in an English atmosphere, and you speak English. When you visit the University, on the other hand, you find all the bottles of the Medical School labelled in German, the inscriptions over the patients' beds in Latin and German, and unless you know Japanese you must speak German to be understood. The Department of Police, again, is modelled entirely upon the French system, and you must speak French there if you are a visitor, and be tried in the French style if you are a prisoner. So I am conducted to a closed door and there told, "It is forbidden by law for any persons except the examining judge and his clerk to be present at the secret preliminary inquiry, but by special permission you may enter." As the proceedings were, of course, in Japanese, I have no difficulty in preserving a perfect discretion. It was simply a very small room with an elevated desk, behind which sat the official and his clerk, closely questioning from a brief before him an individual—a prosecutor, this time—who stood upon the floor. From here we passed, through endless bureaus of busy functionaries, to the several courts, and took seats behind several of the judges in turn. A Japanese court-room at the present moment is a dreary place, but this is only temporary, for the introduction of European laws and European methods of administering them rendered the Old Department of Police entirely inadequate in size and arrangement, and a new one will shortly be completed. The court rooms are very large and square, with plain white walls and board floor. Upon a raised platform occupying one end sits the judge in broadcloth behind a table hung with baize, with a clerk, sometimes in Japanese dress, beside him. In front of the judge and at his feet sit a couple of policemen. Beyond them is a stout railing, behind which the prisoner stands. Then there is the empty floor, and at the opposite side of the room two or three bare benches for the public, but the only occupant of them in each of the courts that I visited was a solitary reporter taking notes. From the animated conversation between the judge and the accused, it was evident, without a word being understood, that the system was purely French. When sentence is pronounced one of the policemen rises and leads the prisoner away to a sort of guard room at the back, in which you can see through the glass door that he winds him up again in the cord and leads him away. In civil cases the benches before the judge are occupied by the counsel, who rise alternately and address him, and so far as one can judge without catching more than a word here and there, they plead with great ease and eloquence. European dress is the rule for the advocates, and one of them who was dressed in the graceful and dignified dress of the Japanese gentleman, and who wore his black hair hanging in a thick mass over his shoulders, was pointed out to me as an extremely clever man and famous as the oddity of the Tōkyō bar.

So anxious were my guides that I should not carry away the impression, as some visitors have done, that I was being shown only half the system, and that the better half, that they took me over every hole and corner of the Department of Police, a huge green and white wooden building surrounding a fountain and pleasant garden court. There was the bureau of the detective force; the bureau of the political police, who look after possible political intrigues, questionable lectures, public meetings, and so forth; the bureau of prostitution; the translators' bureau; the library; the financial auditor's office; the private bank of the department, the temple-like place of detention for political prisoners, the police-barracks and fencing-room, and a score more. After awhile we reached a room where twenty particularly intelligent-looking officials sat at both sides of a long table piled up with newspapers, scissors, blue and red pencils, paste-pots, and all the familiar equipment of the exchange editor's sanctum. I turned to my guides for an explanation and caught them regarding me and each other with amused smiles. Then I saw the joke. It was the Bureau of Newspaper Censorship, and these gentlemen with the spectacles and scissors and paste were examining all the newspapers of Japan for treasonable or seditious sentiments or improper criticism of ministerial and Imperial affairs. I was introduced, and the twenty gentlemen rose simultaneously, and the laugh became general. "This," said my guide, waving his hand proudly over the piles of newspapers and the teapots of the Censors, "is an institution you have not yet reached in England." The procedure of this branch of the Japanese police is simple in the extreme. A lynx-eyed censor discovers an article which seems to his conservative notions to threaten the stability of the Government, to bring a minister into contempt, or to foster improper agitation among the people. He extracts it and submits it to the Director of the Bureau, who probably takes counsel with the higher authorities. If the censor's view is confirmed the editor of the paper is peremptorily but politely summoned—everything is done politely in Japan, and I have no doubt that the schoolboy is politely birched and the criminal politely executed—to appear at the Department of Police at a certain hour on a certain day. When that summons comes to join the innumerable caravan of martyrs to a sense of journalistic duty, he knows that—in the expressive language of the Bowery—he is a "goner." "Sir," he is told, "your estimable journal is suspended for so many days. Good morning." *Voilà tout.* The Bureau of Newspaper Censorship has plagiarized the methods of Fate. It neither warns nor explains nor justifies—it simply strikes. But the Japanese editor is not the least wily of his tribe, and he, too, has taken a leaf from the same book. Noticing how often Fate strikes the wrong person, he has concluded to make the imitation complete in this respect also, and he therefore provides a dummy editor, in the person of some worthy individual who for a small weekly consideration and the attraction of long periods of inactivity, consents to take upon himself the editorial punishment when it comes, for not infrequently imprisonment accompanies suspension. "My friend," says the real editor to the dummy editor some fine morning, "I am about to scarify the Minister of Communications. Pray make your arrangements accordingly. So Justice is satisfied and Japan is guarded and Providence is imitated. But I wonder whether the Censors are not a little puzzled sometimes to know how the illiterate and cheerful individuals who answer their summonses manage to write the subtle and cynical diatribes of which they disapprove. The severity of the Censorship depends, of course, upon the temperament of the Ministers at the time. The other day the publishers and editors of nine Tōkyō papers were imprisoned for a month and fined 25 *yen* for publishing a memorial to the Minister President of *State* against a certain provision of the Constitution, which, the memorialists alleged, virtually set the government above the Emperor!

The Japanese Press Laws are very strict, and suspensions of newspapers and imprisonment of journalists are very common. But a free press is an Anglo-Saxon institution which presupposes, perhaps, more than the Japanese yet possess. " No one doubts," writes a friend of Japan, " that Japanese statesmen would most gladly grant full liberty of speech and pen to their countrymen, but it is certain that to do so would be to expose society to great perils. The class to which Nishino Buntaro, the brutal murderer of Viscount Mori, and Kurushima Tsuneki, the would-be assassin of Count Okuma, belong, does not yet possess sufficient discrimination to safely enjoy such privileges. Irresponsible foreign critics may spin pretty theories from materials furnished by Mill and Spencer, but every practical Japanese statesman with the record of this present year before him must feel that the day for a free press has not yet dawned upon his countrymen."

The whole system of secret police is highly developed in Japan. There is a regular staff of detectives who disguise themselves as labourers, merchants, or travellers, or even in case it is necessary to hunt down some great criminal, hire a house in the suspected neighbourhood, and live there. One of these men loses caste very much in his office, if he does not actually suffer a degradation of position, by failing to return with information he is despatched to secure. Besides these, however, there is a regular staff of private police correspondents in all parts of the country, and one whole bureau at the Department of Police is devoted to receiving, ordering, classifying these, and taking action upon them. A good deal of information must be picked up from the tea-houses, each of which is a centre of gossip, and in one or other of which almost every male well-to-do inhabitant of Tōkyō is an *habitué*. The Yoshiwara, again, is of course a police hunting ground, and the most interesting hour I spent in the Police Department was in conversation with the officials of the bureau which controls this, and in watching the sad and secret spectacle of young girls coming up for permission to enter it as recruits. The whole story and system of the Yoshiwara, however, is so extraordinary, so characteristically Japanese, and so entirely unknown to the rest of the world, that I shall devote a later chapter to it, especially as the police told me that I was the first foreigner who had ever been allowed to investigate it on the spot in the company of the chief of the special Yoshiwara police. To return from this digression to the secret police, I fancy that not only the movements of every Japanese criminal, but of anybody else, Japanese or foreign, that they are interested in, are perfectly well known at the Keishicho. An official of one of the Ministers of State told me that a little while ago he was on a visit to a large town in the south, and met there a foreigner whose movements seemed to him inexplicable on any theory of private life. These suspicions grew, until at last my friend suggested to the Police Department at Tōkyō the advisability of keeping a watch upon the man's actions. A week later a secret report was put into my friend's hands, giving the daily life of the suspect from the time of his arrival. The hour of each

A *Geisha* Dancing.—II.

(*An Instantaneous Photograph.*)

JAPANESE JUSTICE. 75

of his movements, the name of every person with whom he had dealings, the letters he had written, the money he had spent, even the cost of his most private pleasures,—all was put down in black and white. If an Englishman or an American criticizes this system of espionage, the Japanese authorities reply with perfect truth that the Japanese people are different entirely from English or American, and point, besides, to the secret and political police of France and Germany and Russia. In the "rogues' gallery" of Tōkyō alone, I may add, are the *dossiers*, or complete records, of 150,000 criminals, admirably arranged as a card catalogue, like the latest device ot American library cataloguing.

With the exception of the Yoshiwara, of which plenty hereafter, the two prisons of Tōkyō are the most interesting things I have seen in Japan. These are, first, the great prison upon the Island of Ishikawa, at the south of the city, and second, the convict and female prison of Ichigawa, in the centre of the city itself. The former is completely isolated, all communication with the mainland being by police-ferry, and contains two thousand men and boys, all of whom are serving terms of ten years or less. The latter contains fifteen hundred men and one hundred women, among whom are many serving life-sentences. There is a convict-farm attached, and it is here that capital punishment is inflicted. Otherwise the two prisons resemble each other so closely that it is not necessary to distinguish between them in description. Mr. Suzuki, Vice-president of the prison, did me the honours of Ishikawa, and Mr. Adachi, the Director, of Ichigawa.

The entrance is through a massive wooden gateway, into a guard-room, adjoining which are the offices of the Director and officials. The prison itself consists of a score or more of detached one-story buildings, all of wood and some of them merely substantial sheds, under which the rougher labour, like stone-breaking, is performed. The dormitories are enormous wooden cages, the front and part of the back formed of bars as thick as one's arm, before which again is a narrow-covered passage, where the warder on guard walks at night. There is not a particle of furniture or a single article of any kind upon the floor, which is polished till it reflects your body like a mirror. No boot, of course, ever touches it. The thick quilts or *futon*, which constitute everywhere the Japanese bed, are all rolled up and stacked on a broad shelf running round the room overhead. Each dormitory holds ninety-six prisoners, and there is a long row of them. The sanitary arrangements are situated in a little addition at the back, and I was assured that these had not been made pleasant for my inspection. If not, I

ON THE CONVICT FARM.

can only say that in this most important respect a Japanese prison could not well be improved. In fact, the whole dormitory, with its perfect ventilation, its construction of solid, highly-polished wood, in which there is no chance for vermin to harbour, and its combined simplicity and security, is an almost ideal prison structure. Of course the fact that every Japanese, from the Emperor to the coolie, sleeps upon quilts spread out on the floor, greatly simplifies the task of the prison architect in Japan.

On leaving the dormitories we passed a small, isolated square erection, peaked and gabled like a little temple. The door was solemnly unlocked and flung back, and I was motioned to enter. It was the punishment cell, another spotless wooden box, well ventilated, but perfectly dark, and with walls so thick as to render it practically silent. "How many prisoners have been in it during the last month?" I asked. The Director summoned the Chief Warder, and repeated my question to him. "*H'tori mo gozaimasen*—none whatever," was the reply. "What other punishments have you?" "None whatever." "No flogging?" When this question was translated the Director and the little group of officials all laughed together at the bare idea. I could not help wondering whether there was another prison in the world with no method of punishment for two thousand criminals except one dark cell, and that not used for a month. And the recollection of the filthy and suffocating sty used as a punishment cell in the City Prison of San Francisco came upon me like a nausea.

A Japanese prison may be divided into two parts—dormitories and workshops. Of cells or prison buildings properly speaking, there is nothing whatever. It is a place of detention, of reformation, and of profitable labour, and in the latter aspect one of the greatest surprises of life awaited us. Walking across the yard we entered the first workshop, where a couple of hundred prisoners were making machinery and steam boilers. One warder, armed only with a sword, is reckoned for every fifteen men, and here the prisoners were working on contract orders for outside firms, under the supervision of one skilled teacher and one representative of the firm giving the contract. The prisoners work for nine hours a day, and are all dressed in cotton suits of a peculiar terra-cotta or crushed strawberry colour. As we enter, the warder on guard comes to attention and cries, "*Ki wo tsukero*—pay attention!" when all cease work and bow with their foreheads to the floor, remaining in that attitude till a second command bids them rise. They were making large brass and iron steam pumps, and had already turned out seventy this year, and the workshop, with its buzz of machinery and its intelligent labour, would have been exactly like a part of an arsenal here or in Europe, except for the red clothes and the humble prostration. The next shop contained the wood-carvers, and here upwards of a hundred men were squatting with blocks of wood between their knees, carving with the keenest interest upon all sorts of things, from thick simple trays and bowls to fragile and delicate long-legged storks. I bought an admirably-carved tobacco-box, representing the God of Laughter being dragged along by his cloak by six naked boys, and afterwards I asked some Japanese friends who supposed I had picked it up at a curio-dealer's, how much it was worth. They guessed ten *yen*—thirty shillings. I paid sixty-eight *sen* for it—less than two shillings. It is a piece that would be admired anywhere, and yet it was the work of a common burglar, who had made the acquaintance of a carving tool and a prison at the same time. After the carvers came the paper-makers, then the weavers, weaving and dyeing the prison clothing, then the sandal-makers, then the fan-makers, then the lantern-makers, then marvellous basket-work and mats and nets, then an extensive printing-shop, where the proof-reader was a prisoner who had formerly been Secretary of Legation in France, had absconded with one hundred thousand francs, leaving his shoes on the banks of the Seine as evidence of suicide, and eventually been arrested with his mistress at a scene of high jinks in Germany. Then we visited a workshop where

THE PRISON RICE-MILL.

jinrikishas were being made, then one where umbrella-handles were being elaborately carved, then one where every kind of pottery from the rough porous bottle and jar to the egg-shell tea-cup was rolling from a dozen potters' wheels, and then came the great surprise. Two days previous

I had visited the house of the most famous maker in Japan of the exquisite *cloisonné* ware—the enamel in inlaid metal-work upon copper—who rivals in everlasting materials the brush of Turner with his pigments and the pencil of Alma Tadema with his strips of metal. And I had stood for an hour behind him and his pupils, marvelling that the human eye could become so accurate and the human hand so steady, and the human heart so patient. Yet I give my word that here in the prison at Ishikawa sat not six but sixty men, common thieves and burglars and peace-breakers, who knew no more about *cloisonné* before they were sentenced than a Hindoo knows about skates, doing just the same thing—cutting by eye-measurement only the tiny strips of copper to make the outline of a bird's beak or the shading of his wing or the articulations of his toe, sticking these upon the rounded surface of the copper vase, filling up the interstices with pigment, coat upon coat, and firing and filing and polishing it until the finished work was so true and so delicate and so beautiful that nothing except an occasional greater dignity and breadth of design marked the art of the freeman from that of the convict. One simply stood and refused to believe one's eyes.

Fancy the attempt to teach such a thing at Pentonville or Dartmoor or Sing-Sing! When our criminal reaches his prison-home in Tōkyō he is taught to do that at which the limit of his natural faculties is reached. If he can make *cloisonné*, well and good; if not, perhaps he can carve wood or make pottery; if not these, then he can make fans or umbrellas or basket work; if he is not up to any of these then he can make paper or set type, or cast brass or do carpentering; if the limit is still too high for him, down he goes to the rice-mill, and see-saws all day long upon a balanced beam, first raising the stone-weighted end and then letting it down with a great flop into a mortar of rice. But if he cannot even accomplish this poor task regularly, he is given a hammer and left to break stones under a shed with the twenty-nine other men out of two thousand who could not earn anything else.

Prisoners employed at the higher classes of labour are credited with one-tenth of the sum received for their handiwork. But as the work was so good and the running expenses seemed so light, I was much surprised to learn that the prison was not yet self-supporting, only seven-tenths of the total cost being realized from the sale of prisoners' work. Another curious fact is that every adult prisoner is detained for six months after his sentence expires if he is not claimed in the meantime by his friends; and until he is of adult age if he has not reached it and is unclaimed. These prisoners wear blue instead of red after their sentences have expired.

The women's quarter at Ichigaya is separated from the men's by a high wooden fence and gateway guarded by a sentinel, and consists of two or three dormitories and one large comfortable workshop, where all are employed together at labour let out by contract. When I was there they were all hemming silk handkerchiefs, each seated upon the matted floor before a little table, and very neat they all looked, and very pretty some of them, with their loose red gowns and simply-twisted hair. "Those are forgers," said the officer, pointing to three of them; "I do not like them to be so pretty." One of the women had a young baby playing beside her, and another of them as she glanced up at us showed a face entirely different from the rest, pale, sad, and refined, and I saw that her hands were small and very white. It was Hanai Ume, the once famous *geisha* of Tōkyō, famous for her beauty, her *samisen*-playing, her dancing, her pride, and most famous of all for her *affaire d'amour*. Two years ago a man-servant managed to make trouble between herself and her lover, whom she expected to buy her out of the life of a professional musician at anybody's call, and then offered to

WAITING FOR THE CONDEMNED.

make peace again between them on his own terms. So one night she called him out of the house and stabbed him to death with a kitchen-knife. Now music is mute for her, and song is silent, and love is left behind; she will hear no *samisen* again but the prison bell, and of all the merry world around her she will know no more for ever, except so far as she can read the reflection of it as it pales and fades away in the eyes of some companion who may chance to join her for a while.

To the gallows is an easy transition, as it is a natural conclusion. In a secluded part of the grounds at Ichigaya there is a forbidding object like a great black box, raised six feet from the earth at the foot of a long incline cut in the grass. A sloping walk of black boards leads into the box on the left-hand side. The condemned criminal is led up this and finds himself inside upon the drop. The rope is adjusted and the cap fitted, and then at a signal the bottom of the box falls back. Thus the Japanese method is exactly the opposite of our own, the official spectators, including a couple of privileged reporters, being spared the ghastly details of the toilette on the scaffold, and see nothing until an unrecognizable corpse is suddenly flung out and dangles before them. Last year this gallows sent down seven for its tale of men.

IV.

JAPANESE EDUCATION.

IV.

JAPANESE EDUCATION.

"IT is intended," said an official address to the people of Japan issued in 1872 by special order of His Majesty the Emperor, " that henceforth education shall be so diffused that there may not be a village with an ignorant family, nor a family with an ignorant member." And this ideal has been faithfully pursued ever since. But the steep has been a hard one to climb, and the history of the Department of Education shows the constant counter-marching, or rather tacking, by which the goal has been brought nearer and nearer. Boards and Departments and Offices were created and abolished; codes were formulated and repealed; individuals were appointed and dismissed; the very name of every function and the man who filled it has changed half a dozen times. "This was revised in the following year," is a sentence occurring on almost every page of the official records. Elementary education has always been fairly diffused among the Japanese, and it is so rare a thing to find even in the lowest class a man or woman who cannot read and write, that I have no doubt the proportion of illiteracy is higher in Birmingham or in Boston than it is in Tōkyō. When Western aspirations came, however, the old elementary education was no longer good enough for these Yankees of the Pacific, and their difficulties and serpentine course have sprung from a characteristic attempt to combine in one system the Board Schools of England, the High Schools of America, the Normal Schools of France, and the Universities of Germany.

The Japanese educational system exhibits two out of the three great principles of national instruction: it is compulsory and secular. It is not gratuitous. It consists of five parts: Kindergartens, Elementary Schools, Middle Schools, Special Schools, and University.

The Kindergarten is for children between the age of three and six. There are 130 in Japan at present, chiefly in the large towns, without counting the Kindergarten branches of the Elementary Schools, but this number will soon be greatly increased, orders having been issued to governors of Cities and Departments to see that young children attend the Kindergarten, and are not admitted to elementary instruction at an immature age.

The Elementary Schools are of two kinds, Ordinary and Higher. Attendance at the former for thirty-two weeks yearly is compulsory upon all children between six and ten, and Morals, Reading, Writing, Composition, Arithmetic, and Gymnastics, with Drawing and Singing in some cases, are taught. The latter is an optional course of four years more, in which instruction is added in Geography, History, Physics, the English Language, Agriculture, and Commerce. There is also a Simpler Elementary Course of three years for districts so remote or so thinly populated that they cannot bear the expense of the longer course. The comparative shortness of the compulsory term is due to the fact that the country population is a poor one, and yet, owing to the action of Foreign Governments in keeping the hands of Japan tied fast for thirty years to export and import tariffs of nominally 5 and really 3 per cent., the greater part of Japanese revenue has to be unjustly raised by the taxation of the agricultural class. Each school district must be provided with Elementary School accommodation for its children. If there exist a satisfactory private Elementary School, or if some philanthropic individual will endow one, well and good; if not, it must be supported by the school fees, and any deficiency made up out of the local rates. The Simpler Elementary Schools are supported entirely out of the rates. The number of Elementary Schools is 29,233 (of which only 532 are private ones), with 3,233,226 pupils and 97,316 teachers, and the total expenditure upon this branch of instruction last census-year was 8,186,700 *yen* or £1,259,500.

The Middle Schools are also of two classes, Ordinary and Higher. The pupils of the former must be over twelve and have completed the Elementary preparatory course or be prepared to show its equivalent. The course covers five years, and includes such subjects as Ethics, the Japanese Language, Chinese Literature, the First Foreign Language (English), the Second Foreign Language (French or German) or Agriculture,

Geography, History, Mathematics, Natural History, Physics, Chemistry, &c. These schools are designed to prepare pupils either for practical occupations or for the higher educational institutions. Their support may be derived from their own funds or from local taxes. The number of these (including 9 Higher Female Schools) is 132, one (at Osaka) belonging to the Government, 76 to Cities and Departments, 54 to towns and villages, and 2 to private individuals, with 15,100 pupils and 1,060 instructors. The total expenditure upon Ordinary Middle Schools was 417,252 *yen*, £64,193. The weak point in the maintenance of all the foregoing Schools, besides the extraordinary changes to which they have been subjected, is that they are always subject to the success or otherwise of the crops, as the amount of local taxation must be dependent, among a poor agricultural people, upon their yearly prosperity. There is only one cure for this, the accumulation of permanent school funds, and the millionaires of Japan, of whom there are plenty, could not exercise their patriotic generosity in so good a direction as this.

All the foregoing schools are to a considerable extent under popular control, subject to the

Governors of Cities and Departments, whose actions again are directed and strictly prescribed by the regulations of the Department of Education. At this point, however, we enter upon the higher educational system entirely controlled by the central authority.

The Higher Middle School corresponds to the Academical Department of an American University. Candidates for admission must be over 17, and have either completed the Ordinary Middle School course or show its equivalent, and they must bring high testimonials of personal character. The course covers two years and besides advanced studies in the subjects taught before, others such as Latin, Zoölogy, Botany, Geology, Mineralogy, Dynamics, Surveying and Philosophy are added. There is now also a Medical Department of each of these schools, where an efficient Medical Education is given, and Law, Literature, and Engineering may also be added to any school. There are five Higher Middle Schools in Japan, at Tōkyō, Sendai, Osaka, Kanagawa (Yokohama), and Yamaguchi, and the total cost last census-year was 300,000 *yen*, £46,150 equally divided between local taxes and the Department of Education.

It follows that the University is German in its methods, and as I have said elsewhere, after Japanese, German is the language talked there. It consists simply of five "Colleges" for special professional studies, with a degree accompanying graduation in each. These are the Colleges of Law (including Politics), of Medicine, of Engineering, of Literature, and of Science, and so technical is all University work here that this year there were only two graduates from the College of Literature. Candidates for admission must possess a certificate of graduation from one of the Higher Middle Schools or be able to show its equivalent on examination, and the course covers four years for medicine and three years for other subjects. Special students are admitted to an institution called University Hall for a two years' special investigation of some specified subject, for which a degree is given, and there are many loan scholarships for impecunious deserving students. But curiously enough, although the plan is so thoroughly German as regards methods of study and qualification for degrees, the discipline is more strict than in any other country, and the students are treated even more like irresponsible boys than University students are in England. They must reside either in the dormitories or in approved boarding-houses; they can only remain outside bounds until 7 p.m., or 10 p.m. on the night before any holiday; they may wear no dress but the college uniform—a semi-military suit and cap of grey cloth; they may receive no visitors except in the room set apart for the purpose; they may not bring intoxicating liquors into the dormitories or smoke in their bedrooms; the University gates are shut at 11 p.m. and any student not in at that time must present an explanatory letter from one of his sureties before ten o'clock on the following morning; he must provide two solid sureties responsible for him in all matters involving his connection with the University, either of which must be replaced if he is absent from Tōkyō for more than four weeks. The Japanese student, in fact, is not a man in the sense that the American or German student is and is supposed to be, or that the English student generally is without being supposed to be. In his work, indeed, he is a man who would reflect credit on any educational institution, but in his experience he is only a raw youth. He knows nothing of the world; there is nothing in Tōkyō to show it to him except such a "world" as may be viewed through an occasional bit of stolen dissipation at a tea-house ; and his position among his countrymen is so novel that no wonder his head is full of wild notions about society in general and his own particular ability and call to alter it. His manners are usually very bad—worse than any other class of his countrymen. He has especially distinguished himself of late by deliberate acts of flagrant rudeness to foreigners. A partial explanation of all this has been alleged in the fact that "in Japan it usually happens that students from distant provinces, like Kiushiu and Akita, do not see their parents for years in succession. They are thus left absolutely to themselves in the restless capital, and it is little wonder if they grow rough in manners and intemperate in principles. The genial influence of woman, without whom culture is impossible, never beams upon them, and one whole side of their nature is left uncultivated." The students themselves greatly dislike the regulations of the University, and there was almost a riot when they were screwed up to their present strictness five years ago, resulting in over a hundred men being expelled together. "Such rules are a mistake," said one of the students to me loftily; "the good do not need them and the cunning evade them." There is much truth in the remark, and most countries have learned that it is no use having a man at a University unless and until he has learned to take care of himself. Even if the relaxing of the rules should necessitate a stricter standard of admission to the University and a consequent decrease in the number of students, that would be no great evil. It is a broadening of the base of education that Japan needs most; among a people so intelligent and so ambitious as hers there will never be any lack of polishing at its apex. Another significant fact is that the University Calendar (which is a facsimile of the Harvard Catalogue) states the necessary expenses of any student residing in the dormitories or authorised boarding-houses, and including tuition-fee (2½ *yen*, 7s. 6d. per month), cost of living, fire, and light, to range from a maximum of 12 *yen* to a minimum of 7½ *yen* a month—£1 16s. to £1 2s. 6d.! The following are the numbers of students on the roll this year (all the statistics which follow are of 1888) :—

College of Law and Politics 304
College of Medicine 211
College of Engineering 105
College of Literature 36
College of Science 40
University Hall 25

Total (excluding 24 counted more than once) 697

The number of professors and instructors is about 120, of whom 16 are foreigners, and the expenditure upon the University last census-year was 386,935 yen—£59,530. A Japan statistician has calculated that subjects and students in all Japan are related in these proportions :—

Jurisprudence and Literature, 7,578 ; Medicine, 1,568 ; Engineering, Technology, and Art, 1,118; Sciences, 1,694 ; Commerce and Book-keeping, 2,075 ; Agriculture and Dendrology, 895 ; Military and Naval Science and Arts, 1,073 ; Ordinary Education (mostly English), 114,844. These figures relate to male students.

Among Japanese writers the student class receives a good deal of severe criticism. Here is a specimen of intelligent disapproval :—

"Among the 38,114 students of Japan, 6,899 are domiciled in Tōkyō, so that the number of those coming from other localities is 31,215.

Some of these latter look for support to relatives or friends in the capital, but the number of youths having such means of subsistence is extremely small, and steadily decreasing. Most of the students are dependent on their parents or relatives in the country, and are disbursing in the capital money brought from the provinces. The amounts which individual students spend vary from seven or eight *yen* to about fifteen *yen* per month. Taking the average, it may be assumed that each student spends ten *yen* a month, or a hundred and twenty *yen* a year. Thus the total amount of money annually disbursed by these lads is a little over 3,700,000 *yen*. In other words, money aggregating over three millions and a half is being yearly drawn from the provinces to the capital through this channel. What do the provinces receive in return? Nothing, or very nearly nothing, for few of the students ever return to their homes, their sole ambition being to remain in the capital, and there rise to eminence in some walk of life. The few who drift back to their provinces are the worst specimens of the class, lads who, being neither enterprizing nor intelligent enough to join the ambitious race in the city, are not likely to accomplish much in the country either."

But the part of their educational system to which the Japanese attach, and rightly, the greatest importance at the present time, is the detached series of Normal Schools. Plenty of competent and well-trained teachers for Elementary Schools, that is what they need above all things, and that they are in a fair way to secure soon. There is a higher Normal School at Tōkyō, and an Ordinary Normal School in each City and Department. The former educates teachers for the latter, and the latter educates Elementary School teachers. The course is 3 years for the Higher and 4 years for the Ordinary School. Candidates are selected with great care, between the ages of 17 and 20, all their expenses, personal as well as academic, even to their weekly allowance of pocket money, being borne by the State or the public taxes, and in return male graduates of the Normal Schools are under obligation to serve in schools for 10 years after graduation and for three years in any schools to which the Department of Education may appoint them, and female graduates are under similar obligations for five years and two years respectively. There is one Higher Normal School and one Female Normal School at Tōkyō, and 63 in other parts of Japan, of which 14 are for women; the total number of pupils is 6,375 male and 895 female; and the total public expense of this branch last census-year was 612,085 *yen*, or £94,167.

Finally, besides all the foregoing, there are no fewer than 103 special schools, with 583 instructors and 8,913 pupils. Of these 4 belong to the Government, 49 are public and 50 private, and among them may be mentioned the Tōkyō Foreign Language School, the Tōkyō Law School, the Tōkyō Industrial School, the High Commercial School, the Gymnastic Institution, and the Institute of Music. Of the old worthless Miscellaneous Schools over all Japan, which the Department of Education declines to classify, and most of which teach only Japanese and Chinese literature, there are about 1,300.

To complete the picture, however, it is necessary to point out that not a few acute Japanese cities consider there is a fatal flaw in the whole system. "Education in this country," says one of them, "is the exclusive property of the middle classes, specially the *shizoku*. It is rapidly becoming more and more high-class. It is producing a race of scholars who have no property, and does nothing in the way of enlightening the real owners of property. And as for the lower orders, they are lapsing more and more into ignorance."

As regards the spirit of Japanese education, that was summed up for me in three words by H. E. Count Mori, Minister of Education, who has since fallen a victim to the dagger of a conservative fanatic, for some actual or imagined breach of the old religious ceremonial law. "It is our aim," he said, "to inculcate and develop three qualities in our people—obedience, sympathy, and dignity," and I have since found these words recurring like a shibboleth through all the publications of his department. "Obedience," His Excellency added, "because only through obedience come regularity and serenity of life. Our people are irregular at present, and the influence of our rebellion ten years ago has been widespread, for one thing, in making them so. Therefore obedience ranks first among the qualities they need. Sympathy we must inculcate, because it is the crowning virtue of civilization, and the indispensable basis of the democracy we hope, like other nations, to become. Our people have emerged too recently from feudalism to possess sympathy in any great degree, and without sympathy the best man is but a savage. Finally, dignity is the handle of all the blades of character. The Japanese are an impulsive people, and now that they are about to meet the outside world on equal terms for the first time, the value of dignity cannot be over-estimated. These three, again, are the characteristic of an ideal army—invariable obedience, perfect sympathy of high with low, and low with high, equal dignity in victory and in defeat. To aid in their development, therefore, we have established military drill in our schools."

This is how the statesmen of Japan are fulfilling their self-imposed task of educating the nation, and certainly it is an astonishing spectacle of enlightenment and perseverance. Other nations have an educational system which has grown up within them during many years; their common people have been familiar with school needs and school duties from childhood; neighbouring nations furnish a perpetual educational challenge. Japan had none of these advantages. Alone of all the nations of Asia, she determined that her people should have the knowledge of the West and the power that Western knowledge brings, and so she has thrust aside all difficulties in devising and developing her eclectic system and is now supporting it with persistence and generosity which put more than one European nation to shame. Nothing that I have seen in Japan was more striking or more significant than the class of thirty-five girls, from ten to thirteen perhaps, taught by an American lady, writing excellent English on the blackboard, and little Miss Tomita reciting in her low, sweet voice, and with a delicious little foreign accent and pitiful *moue*, "'I am hungry, *very* hungry,' said the spider to the fly." At the University itself I saw in vacation time dozens of young men engaged in independent investigation of abstruse questions in medicine and chemistry and physic; I visited laboratories fitted with apparatus for studying any problem known to the scientific world to-day; I found that in five years' time there will hardly be a position involving high practical scientific knowledge filled by a foreigner in Japan—the architects, the naval architects, the engineers, the mining and railway and sanitary engineers, the chemical and agricultural experts, the physicians and surgeons, the assayers and masters of the mint, all will be the graduates of this Tokei Daigakko; I walked through the great hospital of the Medical School with its long wards and pretty white-robed nurses; and I received a hundredweight of the "Journals" of the different branches of the University, filled with articles in English and French and German on subjects so abstruse and technical that the very titles of many of them were incomprehensible to me. But I always came back to the thought of sweet little Miss Tomita and her *very* hungry spider, as the one thing which implies and promises most for the civilization and the future of Japan.

V.

JAPAN AS AN EASTERN POWER.

V.

JAPAN AS AN EASTERN POWER.

AN OLD WARRIOR.

THE separation of civilization and soldiering has not yet come. Therefore when Japan awoke to Western civilization, she began by the study and adoption of its conscription and its cannon, its tactics and its breechloaders. The result may be classed among the modern wonders of the world. The arsenal of Koishikawa is Woolwich on a smaller scale, with 100 rifles and 70,000 cartridges for its day's work; the dockyard at Yokosuka is not behind Woolwich and Portsmouth in much except size, and first-rate torpedo boats and the most elaborate modern ordnance are turned out there with the regularity of Armstrong or Krupp; the Armstrong cruisers lying off Tōkyō Bay are among the finest vessels of their class afloat, and could make matchwood of many vessels here, and they are manned and officered entirely by Japanese seamen; while the War Department has at least forty thousand men under arms at this moment, and on a declaration of war could put one hundred thousand troops of all arms, and perhaps many more, in the field, with weapons equal to any carried to-day except the latest repeating rifles, all of whom would have served at least a year with the colours, and the majority for three years, and who would make a desperate fight against any army in the world. Yet twenty-five years ago Japanese soldiers wore huge grotesque iron mask helmets to frighten the enemy, chain and lacquer armour to turn his blows, their great shoulder-cannon would have been antiquated in England at the time of the Armada, and they were led by a man with a fan! Of course the Japanese military reorganizers were able to draw upon a large class accustomed to the use of arms, to prepare the way for conscription, and the Japanese have always had a taste for fighting, but after every allowance the rate of progress is simply marvellous.

Is there any reason for this sudden apparition of a Japan in arms? The authorities here think so, and they have received one or two warnings of late that seem to them incentives to continue their efforts. China, who regards Japan as a traitor to Asia (which fortunately she is), is a perpetual anxiety, if not a menace, and in the Riu Kiu (commonly called Loo Choo) Islands and in Korea there have been already misunderstandings of a threatening character, while the question of Chinese immigration, which Japan will have to face as other nations have done, as soon as Treaty Revision comes up for final settlement, looms unpleasantly. Moreover, Japanese statesmen believe that sooner or later somebody will want to take Korea, and they desire to be in a position when that day comes to preserve the neutrality of Japan, or if necessary to offer an alliance to England or the United States, or Russia, or China, as may best suit them, that will decide for ever the mastery of the Pacific. For the Pacific is destined, they know, to be the theatre of great events not very far off, and the Japanese alliance will be the key of the Pacific. It is hardly needful to add that the necessity for an alliance is far more probable for

Japan than the option of neutrality. Her army and navy are therefore well worth the attention of European and American statesmen at this moment, and by the kindness of H. E. Count Oyama, Minister of War, and H. E. Count Saigo, Minister of the Navy, who supplied me with all the official statistics necessary, and afforded me abundant opportunities of personal inspection, I can give what I have reason to believe a completer and more accurate account of the naval and military condition of Japan than has yet been published.

By the abolition of the Daimios, or feudal lords, at the Restoration in 1868, a voluntary and patriotic process which reduced their enormous incomes by 90 per cent., and therefore rendered them unable to maintain any longer their large armies of retainers, the *Samurai*, a proud and well-born class of fighting men, extremely skilled in the use of the terrible Japanese sword, and comprising 10 per cent. of the whole population, found their occupation gone. It was, therefore, easy to enrol them into an army. But although they were born fighters, brave to a fault and faithful to one of the most punctilious codes of honour that has ever been devised, their employment as units of a modern army was attended with this great difficulty, that they found themselves frequently subordinated in position to men who were their social inferiors, and who, except for the uniforms, would have been compelled to pay them every respect. Discipline, therefore, was hard to preserve, and the enrolment of the *Samurai* only served to fill the gap necessarily intervening between the two poles of feudalism and conscription. The latter became law in Japan in 1874, when the modern system may strictly be said to begin. The army regulations were revised and the forces increased by the official edicts of December 28th, 1883, and these constitute, of course with many subsequent alterations and additions, the Japanese military system of to-day.

The first article decrees universal conscription: "Every male inhabitant of the country will be subject to military service from 17 to 40 years of age." The Japanese land forces are divided into *a.* Standing Army; *b.* Standing Army Reserve; *c.* Reserves; *d.* Territorial Army. And the military service thus decreed consists of—

    a. 3 years with the colours, *i.e.*, in the Standing Army.
    b. 4 years in the Standing Army Reserve.
    c. 5 years in the Reserves.
    d. 11 years in the Territorial Army.

The total service being thus theoretically for 23 years—the interval between 17 and 40—but practically for twelve, for while the forces *b.* and *c.* are required to join the colours for sixty days each year, the Territorial Army is called out only in case of war or grave emergency. Special provision is made for men between 17 and 20 possessed of certain educational certificates, corresponding to the French *volontaires* and German *Freiwilligen*, who are permitted to volunteer for one year's service at a time, supporting and clothing themselves. "Should they acquire rapid proficiency," however, the Regulations add, "they may be allowed to quit the ranks after a few months." This seems extraordinary, but exceptional intelligence is so common in Japan—if the paradox be permitted—that allowance is almost always made for it. A conscription rigidly enforced, however, would supply each year far more recruits than the government desires to enrol, the calculation being that 210,000 youths are annually amenable to service. A sweeping system of exemptions was accordingly devised, and this is perhaps the weakest point of the Japanese method, for as has often been remarked in discussing conscription, the more the exemptions, the greater the unpopularity of the service. The following list of exempt persons shows how loosely the net is thrown, and there are many other classes of exemption. (1) All maimed and deformed persons are, of course, permanently exempt, and those who do not reach the prescribed height of 4 ft. 11½ in. are exempt until specially required; (2) one of two brothers simultaneously called on, or a man having a brother already serving; (3) the brother of a man who has died or been permanently disabled while with the colours; (4) heirs of heads of families who are over sixty or who are deformed or otherwise incapable of managing their affairs, and those next in the direct line; (5) heads of families; (6) priests; (7) teachers and professors in public schools or colleges; (8) students of officially recognized educational institutions (this wide exemption dealt an almost fatal blow at private schools); (9) persons whose civil rights have been suspended; (10) persons practising medicine with official diplomas; (11) members of city and prefectural assemblies; (12) government officials whose duties cannot be performed by others. Even after the exemption, however, of these persons and others, comprising in all no less than 40 per cent. of the whole number liable to serve, (in 1887 there were 303,948 exemptions out of a total of 777,972), the number remaining is considerably larger than can be absorbed. A curious and original system of "Supernumeraries" has therefore been invented, under which conscripts drawing supernumerary tickets serve only one year and are then drafted in the ordinary course into the First Reserve of the Standing Army, unless in the meantime they are required to fill vacancies in the regular forces serving with the colours for three years. There is accordingly no fixed number of these "Supernumeraries" at any time, but just as many as remain over in any year from the men called upon the conscription, minus the exemptions, after the regular standing army has been brought up to the number the Minister of War desires to have under arms.

The organization of the Japanese army differs slightly from that of European forces, and therefore I add a brief account of the units of the chief arms. In the infantry, a regiment consists of three battalions of four companies each, and on a peace footing a company is made up of 5 officers, 27 non-commissioned officers, and 160 privates — 192 men of all ranks. On a war footing 80 privates are added, making a total of 272 men. A regiment of infantry on a peace footing consists of 4 commanding officers, 65 officers, 349 non-commissioned officers, and 1,920 privates, in all (including 9 non-combatant officers), 2,347 men, and 12 horses. On a war footing the number of privates is raised to 2,880. In cavalry a battalion on a peace footing comprises 159 men of all ranks and 135 horses, and on a war footing 189 men and 140 horses. In artillery a battery (two of which form a brigade, instead of six as with us) consists of 148 men of all ranks (68 active and 80 reserve) with 86 horses and 4 guns. On a war footing 10 gunners and 2 guns are added. A brigade is thus composed on a peace footing of 1 commanding officer, 11 officers, 51 non-commissioned officers, 240 gunners and 9 non-combatant officers—306 of all ranks with 8 guns and 180 horses. On a war footing this is increased to 326 men with 12 guns and 258 horses. The artillery is armed with $7\frac{1}{2}$ centimetre guns of an Italian model, manufactured at the Japanese arsenal at Osaka.

The Imperial Guard, a picked corps of all

arms, is a distinct force permanently quartered in Tōkyō. In uniform it is distinguished by a red band around the cap, all other troops wearing a yellow one. It is composed of 2 regiments of infantry, 1 battalion of cavalry, 1 brigade of artillery, and 1 company of engineers. Besides the troops of the line and this corps, the Military Academy (Rikugun Daigakko), the Military or Staff College (Shikwan Gakko), and the Gendarmerie are included in the total effective.

The Commander-in-Chief of the Japanese Army is H. I. H. General Prince Arisugawa, the uncle of the Emperor. He is the Director, or President of the General Staff Office (Sanbo Hombu), a body the active functions of which in peace and war correspond to our War Office. The War Department is presided over by H. E. General Count Oyama, Minister of War, and its functions are those of our Horse Guards. That is, the latter collects and organizes the forces, the former directs and uses them. The whole of Japan is divided for military purposes into seven districts, each of which is occupied by one "Legion," or as we should say, one Division, under the command of a General Officer. There are to-day only six foreign officers employed in

A *Geisha* Dancing.—III.

(*An Instantaneous Photograph*).

the Japanese Military Service; two Germans, at the Military Academy; one Frenchman at the Military College; one Frenchman at the Toyama School of Tactics, &c.; one Italian, superintending the making of Ordnance at Yokosuka; and one French bandmaster.

The practical result of the above methods of conscription and organization is a Japanese army of 209,326 men on paper. The following table, which I have compiled from the extremely elaborate and detailed official statistics, shows in simple form all the component parts of this, and their distribution. The statistics are those of 1890, but they give the condition of the forces on December 31, 1887:—

LEGION.	HEAD-QUARTERS.	GEOGRAPHICAL DIVISION.	STRENGTH.	
1	Tōkyō	Capital	9,210	
2	Sendai	North (Main Island)	8,920	
3	Nagoya	East centre	8,267	
4	Osaka	Centre	8,655	
5	Hiroshima	West Centre	7,223	
6	Koumamoto	South	7,476	
7	Yezo (Militia)	North (Island of Yezo)	1,461	
Imperial Guard (Quartered at Tōkyō)			5,591	
				56,803
Military Schools			2,910	
Gendarmes			1,376	
				4,286
Reserves			101,273	
Territorial Army			44,939	
				146,212
Central Staff			2,014	2,014
Total Effective Strength				209,326

The *personnel* of this total is as follows:—

Staff Officers.	Commissioned Officers.	Non-Commissioned Officers.	Rank and File.
450	3,360	10,391	193,804

The proportions of the different arms of the service in Japan, active and reserve, may be seen in the following table (I have omitted the Military Schools, Central Staff, &c.):—

	Active.	Reserve.	Total.
Infantry	38,089	64,293	102,382
Cavalry	671	788	1,459
Artillery	3,817	4,064	7,881
Engineers	1,708	1,814	3,522
Transport	548	54,458	55,006
Gendarmes	1,435	1	1,436
Totals	46,268	125,418	171,686

These are the statistics of 1888, giving the figures of December 31, 1885. It is impossible to compile this table from the figures of 1890. The proportions, however, probably remain about the same.

The number of cavalry shown here is strangely disproportionate. This is probably because it is thought that in military operations in Japan there would be very little scope for this arm, owing to the conformation of the country and the peculiar methods of agriculture. Fifteen hundred mounted men, however, in an army of over 176,000, would surely be quite insufficient to perform the most meagre outpost and escort duties. The cavalry, however, is confined to Tōkyō, and is to be increased at once, I hear, by 2,700 sabres. The enormous disproportion, too, between the active and reserve transport will strike most readers. The one reserve gendarme is, of course, a general officer.

The proportion of conscripts per 1,000 inhabitants is 16·94; of the conscripts themselves only 4·23 per cent. were taken for active service, while 40·59 of the total number were entirely exempted.

I make no attempt here to estimate what actual number of fighting men could be put in the field for this paper strength of 209,326. That is a matter upon which every military expert will have his own theory of shrinkage, and the opinion of anybody else is worthless. The Military Budget for 1889-90 (adding half of the extraordinary expenses for military or naval services), was 13,413,090 *yen*, say £2,063,500, but probably this does not represent much more than two-thirds of the total annual cost of the Military Establishment.

I have left myself comparatively little space to speak of my own impressions of the Japanese

Army. To begin with, Tōkyō is almost as full of soldiers as Metz; there is hardly five minutes in the day when you cannot hear a bugle blown somewhere; mounted orderlies are always trotting about; sentries stand on guard almost as thick as in France; and the groups and troops of young soldiers in their white summer suits and flat German caps, with red or yellow bands, soon become the most familiar objects in the city. The men themselves are neither so short nor so slight nor so well-behaved as I had expected, and their resemblance in dress and face and build to a company of South German recruits was startling at first sight. In their gymnastics, which are very regular and thorough, they are as good as Germans, which is saying a good deal, and when stripped for these they show solidly built, well-developed bodies—exactly what Americans call "stocky." The rigid precision and frequency of their salutes, too, would satisfy a continental martinet. But the one paramount impression that is left by a careful and fairly complete personal examination of the Japanese Army, is its resemblance to similar forces at home. I visited almost every military institution, and inspected every arm of the service, expecting always to find something new to describe—some amusing or picturesque combination of East and West to chronicle. But the expectation was nowhere realized. Everywhere I went and everything I saw—and the statement of this is perhaps the best return I can make to Captain Mouraki who accompanied me, and the commanding officers who so willingly and so courteously turned out their men for my inspection—I found just the same appearance, just the same drill, and just the same discipline as exist at home. I have seen most of the military establishments, and many of the best troops of England and the Continent, and however dull it may seem I can only say that as regards Japan in arms there is nothing whatever new to describe. The Japanese Army, in fact, is a European force, and a body of any arm except the cavalry, which would look small and ill-mounted, might march through any town of continental Europe without being much remarked as foreign troops. The arsenal at Koishikawa, as I have said, is simply Woolwich on a smaller scale, and its English machinery turns out 100 rifles [1] and 30,000 cartridges (70,000 if necessary)

---

[1] As the question of the best rifle is being so widely discussed at present, a detailed account of the Japanese rifle, as

per day, and its artisans manufacture the saddlery and all the rest of the equipment with exactly the same regularity and accuracy. The Military College and Academy are models of such institutions—" One of the foremost of similar institu-

designed from European models by a Japanese colonel, may be of interest. "The calibre is 8 millimetres. There are four grooves, having a depth of a quarter of a millimetre and a constant twist of 1 in 235 millimetres. The breech is closed by a bolt. The mechanism of the repeating portion bears much resemblance to the Lebel system. The magazine, situated under the barrel, contains eight cartridges, and the rifle, when fully loaded, has a ninth cartridge in the breech and a tenth in the chamber. The piece can be used at will as a non-repeater. The sights are graduated up to 2,000 metres of range. The bayonet is a species of dagger, weighing 324 grammes, and having its blade under the stock, in a transverse section. The rifle weighs, without the bayonet, 4·170 kilometres; its length is 1·22 metres. The cartridge weighs 29·78 grammes, and is 75·05 millimetres long; it has a brass socket. The bullet is of hardened lead with a coating of copper; it weighs 15·55 grammes, and is 30 millimetres long. The powder, which produces little smoke and makes little noise, is an invention of the Japanese Artillery Committee; the charge is only 2·2 grammes. An initial velocity of 610 metres is obtained with this charge; the remaining velocity being 250 metres at a distance of 1,000 metres from the muzzle, and of 150 metres at a distance of 2,000 metres. The trajectory being very flat, the bullet is effective throughout a long range. Experiments as to accuracy and penetration have given good results, and shown that the extreme range is about 3,300 metres."

tions which I have seen in the world," I saw that General Grant had written in the visitors' book of one of them. Particularly was this the case at the Toyama College of Tactics, &c., for non-commissioned officers, where I was present at the annual Imperial inspection of platoon firing, firing at moveable targets, fencing, gymnastics, &c., and at the conclusion of which I had the honour of being presented to his Majesty the Emperor. And the barracks of the 2nd Brigade of the Imperial Guard which I visited were just like barracks anywhere else in the world,—a good deal better than many of our wretched barracks in provincial England, allowance being made for certain national differences of food and habits. As for the performances of the troops themselves, I have never seen the infantry manual and platoon exercises done better, and I say this with full recollection of seeing crack Prussian infantry at drill every day for months. The marching and company drill, too, was first-rate. If one made any criticism it would be that the wheeling in line was somewhat unsteady, and that the marching at ease four and six deep through the streets shows all the slovenliness of their French model. The squadron drill of the cavalry was excellent in every respect, and the men's seats particularly good, and their horses particularly well in hand, but the mounts are small and weedy, and therefore this arm is the least effective in appearance. Finally, the battery drill of the artillery as I saw it would be highly creditable anywhere. The two batteries came up at a gallop with perfect steadiness, wheeled, halted, unlimbered, came into "action front," and loaded and fired with a smartness and coolness and rapidity that could hardly be excelled, and that gave evidence of the most thorough and intelligent drill.[1]

Japanese critics, it is fair to add, are by no means invariably enthusiastic or particularly well satisfied on this subject. "The Japanese army was organized," said the *Choya Shimbun* recently,

---

[1] I add one more statistical item from the marvellously detailed and accurate official figures of the Japanese Army, not so much because of the striking character of the fact itself, but also because of the appalling comparison it affords with similar figures concerning our own forces. So far as the army is concerned, it seems certain that public opinion in England on the question here involved must undergo a complete change. The item is this: out of a total number of 32,509 cases of illness in the Japanese Army last census year, only 1,942 were of the nature considered by the Contagious Diseases Act, that is, only 1·05 per cent., reckoning only the non-commissioned officers and rank and file.

"with the idea of being able to put into the field at any moment two hundred thousand troops of all arms, consisting of the men with the colours and the First and Second Reserves. But the strength of the First and Second Reserves at present does not amount to even one half of the

JAPANESE ARTILLERY. "FIRE!"

contemplated establishment, and the cavalry is so deficient in numbers that it does not represent the force required to serve with the colours alone. It is stated that if the three bodies, namely, the troops with the colours and the First and Second Reserves, were moblized to-morrow, barely a hundred and forty thousand men would be found available, and that the military authorities look forward to ten years as the time that must elapse before the original scheme can be fully carried out. Among officers holding high rank, as generals and colonels, some are not acquainted with the systems of strategy and tactics employed in the present era, and among junior officers some have had no actual experience in the field, though their standard of education is high. Sufficient care, too, has not been exercised to devise a system of promotion by merit, and the result is that good soldiers find themselves holding rank inferior to that of men who are by no means their equals in military attainments and capacity. With regard to the private soldiers, there is no doubt that the system of training has the effect of transforming them from rough and uncouth beings into well set-up men with a certain amount of education, and that the new scheme of conscription exercises a beneficial influence on the mass of the nation."

The Japanese Navy calls for much less description than the Army, for its organization and conduct (except a limited conscription) are exactly those of England, English influence and advice having guided its development in every respect. Japanese naval affairs are conducted with great intelligence, and experts assure me that its chief vessels and its dockyards offer almost no opportunity for criticism. With the exception of Captain John Ingles, R.N., naval adviser, the fleet is manned and officered entirely by Japanese. It consisted (in 1887) of thirty-three ships of all classes, ten built in England and fifteen in Japan. A good many of these are now obsolete and comparatively worthless, but, on the other hand, a large number of vessels of all classes are building in England, France, and Japan. One cruiser of the "M" class is building at Yokosuka, one on the Clyde, and one at the Forges et Chantiers; and fifteen torpedo-boats (of the kind that capsized at the French manœuvres) in France. The following six constitute at present the sea-going squadron :—

Name.	Construction.	Displacement Tons.	Horse-Power.	No. of Guns.	Where Built.
Takachiho	Steel	3,650	7,500	8	England
Naniwa	Steel	3,650	7,500	8	England
Foo-sō	Iron-clad	3,717	3,500	6	England
Tsukushi	Steel	1,350	2,400	6	England
Kaimon	Wood	1,358	1,250	7	Japan
Musashi	Composite	1,467	1,600	7	Japan

The first two vessels on this list are the well-known Armstrong cruisers, powerfully armed with two 35 cal. 10-inch guns, six 35 cal. 6-inch guns, two six-pounder quick-firing guns, and a lot of Nordenfeldts, fitted with the very latest and best appliances, and representing a few years ago the highwater mark of naval construction. They show a mean speed of $18\frac{3}{4}$ knots, and can steam 9,000 miles at 13 knots without recoaling. At Yokosuka there are three docks, in length 316, 401, and 513 feet respectively, and at Nagasaki are the best coaling facilities in the East, coal of excellent quality and limitless quantity being conveyed straight from the mines at Takashima and stowed on board by hand with extraordinary speed. Until 1884 the Japanese Navy was recruited entirely from volunteers, but conscription was introduced in that year, and now the proportion of men is 800 volunteers and 280 conscripts. The term of service for the former is seven years, for the latter three years. The *personnel* of all ranks, from the official statistics of 1887 is as follows :—

ASHORE.

Yokosuka Dockyard	3,233
Onohama Dockyard	698
Tōkyō Arsenal	1,082
Tōkyō Powder Factory	268

AFLOAT.

Admirals and officers of corresponding rank	20
Superior officers	189
Officers	625
Midshipmen, &c.	186
Warrant officers	212
Petty officers	1,568
Men	7,504
	10,304

Total of Naval Establishment 15,585

The Naval Budget for 1888-90 (reckoned as before for the Army), reached 6,911,813 *yen*, say £1,063,350. This sum, however, fails to convey an idea of the whole amount Japan is devoting to strengthening her naval establishment. A voluntary contribution fund for coast defence amounted to £406,421, of which the Emperor himself contributed £60,000, and a few weeks after the issue of the estimates for the financial year ending June 30, 1887, a naval loan for no less than 17,000,000 *yen*, say £2,617,000 was announced. Of this large sum, however, only 5,000,000 *yen* has yet been offered to the public, in 5 per cent. Navy Bonds. The expenditure of Japan upon her armament is thus enormous in comparison with her total expenditure (the annual cost of the Army and Navy is 26·52 of the total national expenditure), and there is, of course, in Japan as elsewhere, a Radical political party which strongly protests against it. But as Mr. Trench, then British *chargé d'affaires* in Japan, said in one of his masterly and interesting financial reports to Lord Salisbury, "at a time when all the civilized Powers of the world seem to be vying with each other in enlarging their powers of destruction or defence, it is not strange that Japan should follow the lead thus given, especially when her gigantic and usually lethargic neighbour is displaying an unwonted alacrity and energy in the same direction." The truth is that among her many other lessons from the West, Japan has learned very well that whether or not nowadays those may take who have the power, at any rate only those may keep who can. And she does not mean to lose sight of it.

VI.

ARTS AND CRAFTS IN JAPAN.

VI.

ARTS AND CRAFTS IN JAPAN.

1. AMONG THE TŌKYŌ ARTIFICERS.

THERE is hardly a drawing-room in London or Paris or New York in which there are not objects of Japanese art, and yet not until you reach Japan do you discover what the craze for Japanese "curios" really is. The second thought, if not indeed the first, of almost every globe-trotter who comes to the Land of the Morning, is to procure some Japanese artistic antiquities, either to add to the beauty and interest of his own home or to excite the envy of other collectors. The air is full of talk about "old pieces" and "fine bits" and "magnificent specimens," and when two tourists meet almost the first question they put to each other is " Have you bought much?" Everybody buys something, either new or old, and needless to say in many cases the former passes for the latter. How the new is made, however, and by whom, or what chance there is of finding the old and wherein great value may consists, the vast majority of travellers know nothing whatever. So, as the subject of Japanese art is attracting universal attention at the present moment, and as the stream of travellers is constantly increasing and the prices of all curios therefore rapidly advancing, it may be interesting to throw some light on the above points from one's own personal examination and experience.

In riding about Tōkyō you see a number of shops exhibiting collections of curios and bric-a-brac for sale, but these are fifth-rate dealers to whom no expert buyer ever thinks of going, and their collections are not much above those of our pawn-brokers at home. Real objects of art are never exhibited by the dozen in Japan, either by dealers or private owners. A Japanese gentleman keeps his collection carefully packed away in boxes in cotton-wool, and when he has a guest coming he selects a few according to the time of year, the character of the rooms where he proposes to place them, and what he imagines to be the taste of his guest. A dealer keeps his stock in a fire-proof "go-down" attached to his shop, and when you go to buy he invites you upstairs to a private room, arranges cushions on the floor for you, regales you with tea and sweetmeats, exchanges a series of compliments and small-talk, and after twenty minutes or half an hour he claps his hands and his boys bring the pieces in one by one, extracting each in turn from its box and soft wrapper of old brocade or cloth and setting it before you. Your inspection over, it is delicately wrapped up again. These boxes are beautifully made and are carefully preserved with the inscriptions on them and the wrappers, all of which furnish some evidence of authenticity. The dealer shows you what he likes, and does not seem to care at all whether you buy or not. And it is not much use to ask him to show you any particular objects; the process is a kind of collector's lucky-bag—you must see them as they come out of the warehouse. Nor is it worth while, as you soon discover to your surprise, to bargain with him, except for articles of considerable value. If he shows you a screen for five hundred dollars you might offer him four hundred dollars, and a few days later it might be sent to your house for four hundred and fifty; but you would probably waste your time in offering him forty-five dollars for a lacquer tray priced at fifty. The dishonest dealers are perfectly well known, and few people trade with them except rich travellers who like to be told that the object before them is exactly what they are looking for; while the honest dealers are above suspicion of extortion.

It is equally true of the best modern productions that you cannot see them in quantity anywhere. The makers of them are true artists in spirit, and to see them work you must follow them home and watch them executing commissions. Most of them live on the extreme outskirts of Tōkyō, almost in the country, and each in his little home, with two or three pupils around him, working away under delightful circumstances of life, and under conditions giving the freest scope to his own genius and fancy. The only place that resembled a factory was where *cloisonné* enamel was being made, and this unpleasant reminder of home was only due to the fact that an order for these enamels for the foreign market, sufficient to occupy several years, had recently been received. The process of making *cloisonné* is very complicated. First the plain copper vase or bowl or tray is taken between the knees of the workman, who snips off bits of brass the sixteenth of an inch wide, from a long roll before him, bends them with tweezers and glues them on edge to the copper, thus making the outlines and detail lines of the finished sketch lying before him. An apprentice is putting the simple pattern in this way upon the flat bottom of a tray, while the most skilful workmen is poring over the delicate lines of the eyes and feathers of a cock on a plaque. This outline is next passed to a table between two workmen, who fill up the interstices with enamel, still following the coloured original before them from fifty little cups of coloured pigments. Then the work is fired, again painted with enamels, again fired, and so on, till little is seen but a daub-like distant copy. This is then polished down with the greatest care until the shining edge of the brass strips is reached, and at precisely the same point the colours are a perfect copy of the painting. *Cloisonné* making is labour of the most minute kind added to exquisite skill in the handling and combining of pigments. The result in its highest form is a painting more delicate than water-colours, and more lasting than brass. Formerly only geometrical and decorative designs

THE IVORY-CARVER'S STUDIO. DRAWN BY HIMSELF.

were thus made; now birds and fish and snow scenes have been reached.

An ivory-carver sat in his little room, open to his little garden, chiselling upon a magnificent tusk from which the form of a very graceful female figure was just emerging. The ivory he held between his knees, while his tools were all spread out by his side. "How long will this take you?" I asked. "About four months," he replied. "And what is the proportion between the value of the material and the value of the labour in such a work as this when completed?" "I paid one hundred and forty dollars for this piece of ivory, and four months' work at fifty dollars a month is two hundred dollars. Total cost about three hundred and fifty dollars"—£54. Fancy one of the most skilful and original artificers in the world—for this man's ivories are admired everywhere — simply estimating his own labour at fifty silver dollars—less than £8—a month, while at home our great painters do not hesitate to ask a thousand guineas for a picture covering a few square feet! Is there any doubt which is the true temperament of the artist? "Are you not very sorry sometimes to part with one of these works that has been your companion and part of your life for so long?" He looked up for a moment at a big white lily nodding above him in the garden, and then gently shook his head. "No," he said; "*Kondo no wa motto migoto no tsumori de gozaimasu* ('I expect the next will be more beautiful ')."

The wood-carver, seated with a dozen apprentices among his fragrant litter, knew that we were coming, and presented us each with a large sugar-figured cake in a pretty box. Yet "I am very poor," he said with a smile "for wood-carving is out of fashion now. Nobody builds beautiful Japanese houses any more." He had just been so fortunate, however, as to get a commission for a number of pierced ventilating friezes for the new palace, and one of these he showed to us nearly completed—an exquisitely graceful design of flowers and flying storks. If rich English and Americans only knew for what trifling sums such a man as this Takamura Ko-un would produce for them carved woodwork for their mansions, far more beautiful than they could get elsewhere for ten times—yes, fifty times the cost, he would not be poor long. The sketch on the previous page, which he drew for me, gives but a faint idea of the grace and richness of the completed work.

The most interesting and elaborate process is lacquer making, and its results, both new and old, form a majority of the art-products of Japan, as it has been the most characteristic and popular Japanese art for 1,500 or perhaps 2,000 years. It is so elaborate that I can give only the most meagre outline of it. The object, generally a tray, a box, or a cabinet, is first made in thin white pine as only Japanese carpenters can make such things; then the joints are all covered with muslin and rice glue and a thin coat of lacquer, and the whole is dried in the oven. Lacquer is the sap of the lacquer-tree, *Rhus vernicifera*, drawn off by making incisions in the bark during the rainy season, and secretly prepared. Then thin hemp cloth is stretched tightly over the whole surface, upon a basis of mixed lacquer and wheat-flour. Then coat after coat of different kinds of lacquer is laid on, polishing after polishing is given, till after the last coat the last polish is attained with powered calcined deer's horn applied with the finger. The gold mottled surface is produced by dusting gold flake through a muslin sieve, and the designs upon coloured lacquer are first traced on in gold and then the powders are applied in a multitude of ways, from the brushes of rat's hair and hare's hair and cat's hair and human hair, and hair from the long winter coat of a horse, to the simple pad of cotton-wool. Old gold lacquer is so extremely costly, the artificer told us, because of the large quantity of gold used to obtain the right surface. "The price of this box, which I have just finished," he said, showing us a wonderful specimen of gold lacquer design in cherry-blossoms and trees, with a river and houses in the distance, "is three hundred dollars and it has been eight months in hand. If I had made it as they made the old lacquer it would cost six hundred dollars, but there would be no market for it."

As regards the antiquity of the lacquer industry, Japanese chronicles give the name of the person who was "Chief of the Imperial Lacquer Department" under the Emperor Kō-an, in the year B.C. 392. In the seventh century A.D. lacquered articles were received in lieu of taxes, and afterwards, so great was the value set upon lacquer for the Emperor's own use, that the making of it except in the Imperial Lacquer Department was prohibited. In the eighth century, as enough lacquer could no longer be procured from the wild trees, every farmer was compelled, first, to plant from forty to eighty lacquer trees, and second, to pay his taxes in lacquer. Now, lacquer trees grow everywhere, as they are very hardy. The oldest piece of lacquer-work extant is a box which held the scarf of a Buddhist priest who lived in A.D. 540. It seems highly probable that if working in lacquer—I mean work of the straightforward and cheap kind—was understood and could be practised in other countries, it would be found applicable to an infinite number of useful purposes. For example, experiments have recently been made to determine whether a coating of lacquer will not prove a perfect covering for a ship's bottom.

The actual manual skill of the Japanese artifice, seems remarkable to us, but it does not strike his fellow-countrymen as being much out of the common. And, indeed, the traveller in Japan soon learns to transfer his wonder from the individual to the nation. This extraordinary people who pull the saw or the plane towards them instead of pushing it away, who make the threads of their screws run the other way from ours, who sit down in the presence of a superior as a mark of respect, who blow their noses upon paper and wrap their parcels in pocket-handkerchiefs, are born with a manual dexterity that is simply astonishing. This is true of everybody, men and women, low and high alike. Your *jinrikisha* coolie will tie knots, repair his vehicle, or lend a hand in anything you are doing, with the knack of a man-of-war's man and the delicacy of a dentist; the cook at the house where I am staying will knock off charming little sketches for the children by the hour; and any little job that requires intelligence and manual skill almost any Japanese will do for you. To give only one example, if you happen to be suffering from that troublesome and painful infliction, a boil, your Japanese servant will take a hair, pass it by some magic known only to himself, round the inside of the sore and with only a twinge to yourself remove the whole of the diseased flesh. What the ordinary Japanese most enjoys in his works of art is the quaint or comic telling of a story or depicting of a humorous incident. The carving of the man carefully lifting the box which he has put down over a rat, and waiting with uplifted club to smash it as it comes out, while the rat, having eaten away a corner, has escaped up his sleeve and is sitting on his back watching the process over his shoulder—that is the spirit which appeals to their fancy. I have taken a great many photographs in Japan of all sorts of people, instantaneous street-views, studies of dancers and portraits of *geisha*, and although some of them seemed to me rather interesting, my Japanese friends did not care for them at all. But one day I took a picture of a very pretty girl with her arm round a large carved wooden *Daruma*— an effigy of the saint who squatted in such a prolonged inward contemplation of the nature of things that his legs rotted off—and looking teasingly into his face with an appealing look, while his fixed gaze over her head seems to be an appeal for help against the temptress. And over this picture at last my friends were enthusiastic. "That is excellent," they said, "it is delightful—*it is Japanese!*" Actually the fame of this photograph reached the reporters, and a paragraph appeared in the newspapers congratulating me upon it, and giving the name of the owner of the *Daruma*—a very sedate person—who was by no means grateful for notoriety of that particular kind. The picture forms the frontispiece of this volume.

As soon as the Treaty Revision question is settled, and it is easy for Japanese and foreigners to work in partnership, there will be an extremely interesting and profitable opportunity for the proper organization of these artificers and the development and direction of this national dexterity. At present they produce very little in amount, that little is snapped up eagerly by those on the spot, the producers remain poor, and their ideas are the same from generation to generation. But in such fields as wood-carving for house decoration, the making of fine furniture with decorative carving, the casting and chiselling of copper and silver and gold articles for the table, the weaving of splendid brocades for hangings and curtains, the making of exquisite porcelain articles for table service—in all these and many other directions there will be limitless opportunities for Japan to supply the Western world with beautiful and useful objects, to her own profit and their education and delight. To get anything of this sort made now it is necessary first of all to find out a man who can make it—no easy task, for the individual artificers are known only to a very small circle; then you have to teach him exactly what it is you want; and finally you have to wait months and months before you can get it. I saw a silver teapot the other day, beautifully chiselled and beaten out of very heavy silver after an old Chinese design—a masterpiece of the silversmith's art. But when I expressed a wish to give an order for a somewhat similar article, I was told that it would be between eighteen months and two years before it would be finished! If the chief artificers of these arts could be brought into one organization, directed by a competent foreigner, taught Western needs and preferences, and yet left absolutely free to follow out their own artistic inspirations, both Japan and the world would be the gainers. The Eastern market for furniture alone is so extensive and profitable that a large and prosperous firm has grown up in

Shanghai, employing Chinese workmen. Yet this is one of the things that the Japanese would do infinitely better. The great danger, of course, in such a scheme, will be that the genius of the Japanese artificer may not be able to resist the degrading influences of even a distant approach to the factory system. It will be an interesting problem to watch.

VII.

ARTS AND CRAFTS IN JAPAN.

VII.

ARTS AND CRAFTS IN JAPAN.

II. PAST AND PRESENT.

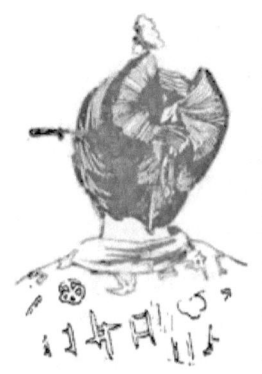

IT is easy enough to write of the curio-shops of Japan and of the odd manners and customs of the dealers in artistic antiquities, but it is a very different matter when you come to the curios themselves. This is a subject upon which only an expert, who has found wisdom by years of experience, and the wasting of a small fortune in learning not to make mistakes, has the right to an opinion. Now, Captain Brinkley, R.A., of whom I have written in my letter on Japanese journalism, is the first living authority upon Japanese and the Chinese porcelain, and he has been one of the closest students for many years of other branches of Japanese art, though he is careful not to claim expertship in them. For twenty years he has collected here and in China, and his overflow collections, one of which, called "The Brinkley Collection," was dispersed in New York a few years ago, are famous among connoisseurs everywhere. Collectors come to him with letters from all parts of the civilized world, and only a few days ago one of them, an American millionaire, was begging to buy a few of his pieces—"so that I can say I have some bits from your collection, you know." The work of his life, a "History of Chinese and Japanese Keramics," with a multitude of the most beautiful water-colour book-illustrations I have ever seen, is nearly ready for the publishers. The following very interesting "true truths" about Japanese curios, old and new—their makers, honest and dishonest—and their buyers, wise and foolish, I owe to Captain Brinkley. Collectors will do well to lay them to heart.

"The hopeless decadence of Japanese Art," is a favourite phrase among connoisseurs in Europe. That opinion is due partly to the natural tendency of collectors, who are always *laudatores temporis acti*—and partly—perhaps chiefly—to the misrepresentation of dealers, who seek to enhance the value of old pieces. Some lapse from the best standards was inevitable, but it is not such a lapse as M. Louis Gonse would lead us to suppose when he speaks of "the wretched modern products of Japanese art, so feeble in every way." With the fall of feudalism in 1868, Japanese art manufactures lost the most liberal and eager patrons ever developed by any social conditions anywhere. Each feudal king was a chief who based the reputation of his fief on martial prowess, up to the time of the *Taikō*, and on industrial superiority after that time. Specimens of the art products of the principal fiefs used to be sent periodically to the Shōgun's Court in Yedo (Tōkyō) and to the Imperial Court in Kyōtō. Between the *Daimyo* themselves, also, there was a constant interchange of objects of art. Thus, whenever one of the artist artisans, who constituted a class peculiar to Japan, developed any special ability, he could count on the munificent patronage of his feudal lord. His future was thenceforth assured. He became a pensioner, working leisurely and giving full play to his genius, certain that excellent results would always guarantee him against any inconvenient scrutiny as to the expenditure of time or money. When feudalism was abolished, these halcyon days disappeared. Men depending on art industries for a livelihood were compelled to turn temporarily to foreign markets, and as a natural consequence they adapted themselves to the supposed requirements of those markets. To appreciate what this meant, one need only recall the attitude of the popular mind thirty years ago in England, for example, towards all questions of æsthetics. The Japanese soon fell into the notion that profusion of ornament, elaboration of detail and decorative brilliancy, were the first essentials of a successful appeal to Western approval. Hence the production of a host of objects meretricious, gaudy and vulgar, representing not Japanese taste, but a Japanese conception of foreign taste. This was the Brummagem period of Japan's art. Happily she soon emerged from it. For some years past her great aim has been to return to her own canons, and she now manufactures objects worthy of comparison with the choicest masterpieces of former times.

This is, perhaps, not true of all branches of art, but it is certainly true of art manufactures. In pictorial art it might be rash to say that Japan possesses just now any masters worthy to rank with the celebrities of past ages. She has no Sesshiu, no Motonobu, no Sosen, and no Okyo. She has, perhaps, a Hokusai, and a Tsunenobu, but one hesitates to pronounce a confident dictum on this point. In respect of general excellence, however, her painters are not below the average level of the past, though they certainly do not reach its highest eminences. Undoubtedly Kyōsai can paint a crow as well as Chokuan ever depicted a hawk, and some of Kangyo's landscapes deserve to be hung side by side with those of Tanyu. If, however, a collector were to assume that the porcelains, lacquers, bronzes, and ivories, now offered for sale in Japanese shops, are virtually equal to the corresponding works of past years, his assumption would be too large. Let us examine the matter a little in detail. In the Keramic industry for example, there is certainly a loss, or at least a practical absence, of technical ability. This is evident in two respects: first, in the purity and fineness of porcelain *pâte*, and secondly in the brilliancy and quality of vitrifiable enamels used for surface decoration. Why there should be difficulty, apparently insurmountable, in obtaining a *pâte* equal to that of former times, no one pretends to explain exactly. Chemically considered there are six distinct varieties of porcelain in Japan, but for the present purpose it is enough to speak of the two great centres of production, Arita and Owari. The porcelain of the former contains, in a hundred parts, seventy-seven of silica and eighteen of alumina; the porcelain of the latter, seventy of silica and twenty-one of alumina. The Arita (Hizen) porcelain differs from all other porcelains in being manufactured directly from the stone of Izumiyama. Elsewhere porcelain *pâtes* are obtained by mixing a fusible and an infusible element—*Petuntse* and *Kaolin*—the "bone" and "flesh" of the ware. But in Hizen nature has provided material ready to be employed without any admixture. This dispensation, a source of much pride to the potters of the district in olden times, has its disadvantages as well as its advantages. The manipulation of the stone demands immense care and skill. Success depends, in a great degree, upon an unsparing expenditure of labour and expertness. In Owari, on the contrary, the usual process is followed; the porcelain stone is mixed with a *Kaolin* clay. Both stone and clay are procurable in almost unlimited quantities, but their composition is so variable that the action of the mass in the presence of a high temperature is a matter of the greatest uncertainty. The Owari potter, not yet sufficiently scientific to analyse his materials, trusts much to chance, and consequently devotes a minimum of labour to preliminary processes, which, for aught he knows, may be ultimately thrown away. Owari now produces nearly all the blue-and-white porcelain of Japan, besides quantities of ware subsequently decorated with pigments and enamels in the *ateliers* of Yokohama and Tōkyō. Arita produces the bulk of the enamelled porcelain. At neither place can the workmen afford to prepare their *pâtes* with the loving care bestowed in former times. Probably the *finesse* of the process has escaped them through want of practice. At all events, the results obtained are decidedly inferior. So, too, of decorative enamels, though in a much less marked degree. The preparation of these is often imperfect, and there is always a disposition to replace them with pigments. This latter tendency belongs to a more serious class of faults. Crude, gritty *pâte* is bad technique, but the use of pigments for surface decoration is bad art. It must be remembered that the item of decorative designs enters into the account, and here the advantage is on the side of modern Keramists. They choose their subjects from a wider field, and execute them with no less fidelity than their predecessors. Besides, porcelain proper has always been a secondary product of the Keramic industry in this country. In faience the Japanese have achieved and still achieve their greatest triumphs. Probably the most æsthetic outcome of the potter's art in any country was the celebrated Satsuma faience. In the manufacture of this beautiful ware the workmen of former times far excelled those of the present generation. But if you go to Kyōtō, you will find Tanzan, Dohachi, Seifu, and Kanzan turning out faience which, in respect of technique and artistic qualities alike, is certainly not inferior to the old-time *chefs-d'œuvre* of Awata, Iwakura, and Kiyomizu. The Satsuma faience of former times excelled so signally in beauty of *pâte*. Its exquisitely mellow, ivory-like surface, with crackle almost imperceptibly fine but perfectly regular, and lustre rich yet sufficiently subdued to suggest a restful air of solidity, offered an ideal ground for the delightful harmonies in gold, silver, red, green, and blue, so cleverly chosen by the Satsuma potter. It is not impossible now to reproduce the same delicacy, wealth, and chasteness of decoration, but the incomparable *pâte* is seen no more. It is probably understood by very few Western collectors. Yet, strangely enough, "old Satsuma" has always been a sort of craze in Europe. I say "strangely," because the great majority of its devotees cannot have any practical acquaintance with the ware. They must have simply followed the fashion. Genuine examples of old Satsuma have always been rare as choice diamonds. During the past ten years, the average number of pieces coming into the market has not exceeded ten or twelve. Thousands, however, have been sent to Europe. Stained with chemicals and otherwise disfigured to simulate age, they have educated a very false idea of *Satsumayaki* among average connoisseurs. Inexperienced collectors would do well to remember that there are no large, highly decorated specimens of genuine old Satsuma in existence. Big vases, censers, and jars, bedizened with armies of saints, peacocks, and historical scenes, are attractive ornaments in their way, but they have nothing in common with old Satsuma.

The Japanese are past masters of the art of

manufacturing ancient specimens. All the familiar devices of burying in the ground, exposing on the roof, steeping in tea or decoctions of *yasha*, begriming with fumes of incense, and so forth, are now thrown into the shade by a Yokohama artist, and a great potter at that, who actually simulates marks of age in manufacturing a piece, and fixes them in the furnace. Such tricks will flourish so long as the folly of collectors induces them to value age for its own sake. It is difficult to understand the motive of such infatuation. Of course in the products of every country there are specimens which, though not pleasing from either an artistic or a decorative point of view, possess interest as links in the historical chain of industrial development. But this is a question quite outside the ordinary collector's domain. The points of attraction for him are practically limited to beauties of skilled technique or artistic conception. He ought, therefore, to recognise that marks of age are emphatically a blemish, and that, so far from augmenting, they seriously diminish, the value of a Keramic specimen. Japanese *virtuosi* have always understood this. They preserve choice vases and censers wrapped in silk or brocades and enclosed in nests of boxes.

A *Geisha* Dancing.—IV.

(*An Instantaneous Photograph.*)

Every scratch, every stain, they regard as a defect, and by periodical washings they keep their treasures pure and bright. As a rule there is a period of greatest excellence for each class of ware. Sometimes it is a remote period; sometimes a more modern. Thus, while an example of "Famille Verte" of the *Kanghsi* (1661-1722) era is finer, in many respects, than a similar price of the *Lungching* or *Wan-li* time (1567-1620), the converse is true of yellow monochromes; and while Owari blue-and-white dating from the middle of this century far excels its predecessors of the same factory, one must go much further back to find choice examples of the same style in Imari porcelain. Apart from the place occupied by a particular epoch in respect of artistic or technical excellence, there is not the smallest reason to look for age in a Keramic specimen, and if collectors would make up their minds to regard marks of antiquity as tokens to awaken distrust rather than to excite admiration, they would at once close the path to a multitude of deceptions.

Other art manufactures, speaking generally, are in a condition of high development. China, in her palmiest days, never produced *cloisonné* enamels comparable with those now made in Japan. No country indeed, ever manufactured anything showing such a combination of wonderful manual dexterity and decorative instinct. Moreover, this industry is virtually a new departure. Mr. Audsley, in his stupendous work on "The Ornamental Arts of Japan," has been betrayed into singular errors as to the history of Japanese *cloisonné*. In feudal times the productions of Japanese workers in enamel were insignificant and unattractive. The art had no recognised status and its outcome was deservedly neglected. But a few years after the opening of Japan to foreign trade, the prices commanded by old Chinese enamels in Western markets led enterprising Japanese artists to turn their attention in this direction. They were encouraged by foreign speculators, and the result was that between 1865 and 1872, quite a large number of imposing vases, plaques, censers, and so forth, found their way to Europe. They were sombre pieces, defective in colour, but showing elaborate workmanship, and their manufacturers did not hesitate to employ whatever decorative designs were likely to increase the vicarious dignity of a piece. The sixteen-petalled Chrysanthemum and the five-foil Pawlownia figured profusely on vessels innocent of the remotest relation to the Imperial family. Of these specimens a number came into the hands of some English collectors, and Mr. Audsley devotes pages to their description and classification. His thesis reads like a huge jest. One of his preliminary embarrassments was that such pieces had never been seen before. Their types were not to be met with in any of the known museums, at Leyden, at the Hague, in Munich, in Dresden, in London, or in private collections of note. Mr. Audsley was driven to conclude that the European "knowledge of an ancient and apparently extinct school of Japanese enamelling dated from 1865," and that "in England alone were the dignity and importance of the industry properly recognised." Of all conceivable hypotheses, the only one he did not happen upon was that the "school" itself dated from 1865. "All the Japanese who had an opportunity of inspecting the enamels in England pleaded entire ignorance regarding them; said that they had never met with them in Japan, and appeared somewhat surprised to know that they had come thence." But Mr. Audsley was not disturbed. Fixed in the belief that the enamels were ancient it only remained to account for their sudden emergence into the light of appreciation and connoisseurship. By a process of negative reasoning he arrived at the conclusion that not being this and not being that, they must be the other. So at last they became temple furniture centuries old, and the result is that in the beautifully executed plates of his book a series of almost entirely modern manufactures is carefully divided into three periods, dating from the fifteenth to the nineteenth century. One cannot too much regret that works so imposing and attractive as "The Ornamental Arts of Japan" should form the gospel of English collectors. So long as authors with Mr. Audsley's opportunities circulate such singular misconceptions—attributing to ancient factories and Buddhistic patronage enamels that were produced in recent years solely for the foreign market, under the direction of a speculative Hebrew, and ascribe to a Kakiemon of the seventeenth century and to Kenzan of the eighteenth, porcelain and faience statuettes of entirely recent manufacture—so long will false notions of Japanese art prevail in the West, and so long will the trade of the adept forger flourish.

In one direction, modern Japanese enamels

have reached their acme of development. It is impossible to conceive higher efforts of technical skill and elaborate accuracy than the enamels of Kyōtō. But in Tōkyō a new departure was made a few years ago. The artists conceived the idea of producing pictures in enamel. In these enamels the cloisons are hidden, as far as possible. You have a wide field of delicate colour—generally relieved by gradations of tint—forming the ground for landscapes, floral decoration, snow scenes, and so forth, effects of aërial perspective and chiaroscuro being obtained with marvellous skill. Whether the canons of true art are strictly observed in such work may be a question. The results achieved are certainly most beautiful, but the best designers are not employed, and a higher stage is evidently attainable. Belonging to the same category as these wonderful enamels are some of the modern embroideries of Kyōtō. In that city you find experts who paint with their needles. Their best works are scarcely distinguishable from pictures on canvas or silk. There seems to be no limit to the capacity of the Japanese art artisan. If his genius can survive organization a wide vista of industrial triumphs lies before him. In other branches also, glyptic art and metal work for example, he gives similar promise of success. His modern bronzes and his iron inlaid with gold and silver are remarkable accomplishments. As in pictorial art, so also in metal work, certain epochs were happy in the possession of great masters. From the time when his sword and his armour ceased to be the first objects of a Japanese gentleman's concern, the field for workers in metal was immensely narrowed. We shall never, perhaps, see again those extraordinary miniatures in metal that are found on the sword-furniture of former times. But the ability that conceived and executed these marvels is not lost: it has only been diverted. You see unmistakable evidences of its existence and full exercise in the metal work of to-day. So, too, of carving in wood and ivory. There are glyptic artists of the utmost excellence. None of the masterpieces of their predecessors put them to blush. It is true that large quantities of wood and ivory carvings are exported which present no commendable features of any kind. The majority of Western collectors buy these much as they would buy chairs or tables. No matter whether there is any display of the artist's feeling or the modeller's skill—it is enough that the objects represent a great deal of labour, a certain amount of bizarre vigour, and a phase of Japanese fancy. You can go to shops in Yokohama and see ivory carvings of this class ranged upon shelves by scores and hundreds. The mechanical repetition of such toys is a steadily degrading influence. Happily, however, there are artists who refuse to prostitute their talents to the wholesale demand of upholsterers and exporters. Among their works the patron and lover of true art will find no lack of exquisite objects. The tourist visiting Japan with a full purse would be wiser than his class to collect only the honest and beautiful products of her modern art, instead of encouraging forgeries and deceiving himself by running after specimens which, in nine hundred and ninety-nine cases out of every thousand, are inferior examples of new work, disfigured by simulated marks of use and wear.

VIII.
JAPANESE WOMEN.

VIII.

JAPANESE WOMEN.

THE Japanese woman is the crown of the charm of Japan. In the noble lady and her frailest and most unfortunate sister alike there is an indefinable something which is fascinating at first sight and grows only more pleasing on acquaintance, so that the very last thing to fade from the memory of anybody who has been fortunate enough to linger in Japan, must be these

"— bright vestures, faces fair,
Long eyes and closely braided hair."

Good looks are not enough to account for this;

prettiness is the rule among Japanese women, but I think the charm lies chiefly—though to attempt a rough-and-ready analysis is like dissecting a humming-bird with a hatchet—in an inborn gentleness and tenderness and sympathy, the most womanly of all qualities, combined with what the Romans used to call "a certain propriety" of thought and demeanour, and used to admire so much. If you could take the light from the eyes of a Sister of Mercy at her gracious task, the smile of a maiden looking over the seas for her lover, and the heart of an unspoiled child, and materialize them into a winsome and healthy little body, crowned with a mass of jet-black hair and dressed in bright rustling silks, you would have the typical Japanese woman. To write of her life and thoughts and habits and future developments, one must show much temerity, or else be with "divine affection bold," but there is so much to say, and she will play so important a part in the final civilizing of Japan, that I must try.

The key to the character of the Japanese woman lies in the word obedience. Ages ago her "three great duties" were religiously declared to be obedience; if a daughter, to her father, if a wife, to her husband, if a widow, to her eldest son. "The kid drinks its milk kneeling," says the Japanese proverb—even the brutes show respect to their parents. So at the will of her parents the Japanese girl accepts her husband or joins the slaves of Aphrodite, and Confucius is presumably happy at the devotion to his behests. Her education consists of reading and writing, the polite accomplishments of dancing and playing on the *samisen* and *koto*, the reading of the polite literature of poetry, the tea-ceremonial, *cha-no-yu*, and the flower-ceremonial—all very civilizing studies, but involving no development of character. Dancing plays a very important part in the education of both boys and girls. In good families the dancing teacher comes every other day, regular practice is an affair of routine, and private entertainments where the children perform are arranged by friendly families. This education is that of the upper classes; for the middle and lower classes obvious deductions must be made from it. At last — or rather very soon — comes the wedding day, and the girl doffs her bright scarlet under-garment. How far this festival is supposed by the Japanese themselves to coincide with the slaking of the "burning desert-thirst" of personal passion, which the western nations more or less hypocritically attribute to that day of days, is revealed by their proverb—the universal one in a prettier form — " Love leaves with the red petticoat."

The days when a Japanese wife stained her teeth black on her wedding day and shaved her eyebrows when the first baby was born, are past, except perhaps among the lower classes in remote country districts, but the Frenchwoman's remark, making due allowance for its exaggeration, may be repeated by the women of Japan— "fille, on nous supprime; femme, on nous opprime." The expression *res angusta domi* might have been invented for Japan, so narrow of necessity is the wife's home life. The husband mixes with the world, the wife does not; the husband has been somewhat inspired and his thoughts widened by his intercourse with foreigners, the wife has not met them; the husband has more or less acquaintance with Western learning, the wife has none. Affection between the two, within the limits which unequal intellectuality ruthlessly prescribes, there well may be, but the love which comes of a perfect intimacy of mutual knowledge and common aspiration, there can rarely be. " A companion in solitude, a father in advice, a mother in all seasons of distress, a rest in passing through life's wilderness "—such an ideal of wifehood is virtually impossible. The ghost of Confucius forbids, and until that is exorcised, it will remain impossible. The very vocabulary of romantic love does not exist in

EN DÉSHABILLÉ.

Japanese—*à fortiori*, there is little of the fact. You could not translate the love-letters of Abelard or Fichte into Japanese.

An example may illustrate this. A young Japanese nobleman of my acquaintance, holding a subordinate official position, recently became desperately enamoured of a girl whom he met in the country. He brought her to Tōkyō and installed her in a separate establishment. His wife, however, and mother-in-law discovered the *liaison*, great family jars ensued, paragraphs appeared in the papers, and his friends feared that the scandal would result in the loss of his official position. A compromise was therefore effected, by which he gives up the establishment, his wife and mother-in-law cease from troubling, the girl returns to her home in the country, and comes to stay at his house once a month, thus (asking Mr. John Morley's pardon for the paraphrase) "adding to the gratification of physical appetite the grotesque luxury of domestic unction."

Marriage is a civil contract, without religious or official ceremony. The ceremonies, which are elaborate, are confined to the families and friends of the contracting parties, and the legal recognition takes the form of registration in the government records. Divorce again—the *pis aller* of marriage—is theoretically easier in Japan than in Chicago, but as a matter of fact the intervention of the families protects the wife from injustice or caprice in all cases where husband and wife are respectable enough to have any family ties at all.

The higher you ascend socially the more hostile and influential are the forces arrayed against divorce. A woman may also sue for a divorce from her husband. As for polygamy, I take the following statement from a high authority:—
"Strictly speaking polygamy is not practised in Japan at present. Indeed, it has never been legal; the law acknowledges only one wife. But concubinage is not uncommon. In many respectable households there is a concubine—perhaps two or even three—in addition to the wife, a miserable state of affairs, degrading, unhappy, and mediæval. Already the reform advocated by the Kyôfû-Kai has been quietly but resolutely put into practice in the circles that represent modern Japan. To the honour of the official classes, of the nobles, and of the leading merchants, it must be recorded that, with few exceptions, concubinage is no longer practised, and has come to be regarded as inconsistent with civilization. Whether public opinion is ripe for the criminal condemnation of the custom, we cannot pretend to say." [1] One of the vernacular newspapers commented on the above in a characteristic Japanese fashion. It wrote:—" Monogamy has been the law of Japan

[1] *Japan Weekly Mail*, June 15th, 1889.

from ancient times. We have not yet heard that the system of polygamy is adopted. Concubinage alone exists. By all means let concubinage be abolished, but remember that each country has its own customs and habits. Nothing is gained by importing exotic fashions. Even though laws were framed to enforce the system of monogamy, if, as is the case in Western lands, adultery became prevalent, we should have the pretty name of monogamy indeed, but the reality would be ugly. For our own part, we don't believe that everything is above reproach in the Christian marriage system."

Notwithstanding all the foregoing, however, the position of the Japanese wife is higher than in any other Oriental country. She is addressed as *O-ku-sama*, "the honourable lady of the house," and as a rule every consideration is accorded to her. Because of the innate gentleness of the people and their elaborate and rigorous etiquette, the relations of husband and wife are far easier and happier than the actual facts regulating them would lead one to suppose. The wife is faithful to a fault, and adultery on her part is almost unknown. But the complete civilization of Japan waits for the enlightenment and greater safeguarding of its women.

It must be distinctly understood that in writing the above about Japanese women and wives, I have had in view chiefly the upper class of the generation that is, and that even in this there are many examples—among the Ministers, for instance—of husband and wife living on precisely the terms of English or American upper-class couples. The generation that is growing up will be very different. Not only will the men of it be more Western, but the women also. As girls they will have been to schools like our schools at home; they will have learned English and history and geography and science and foreign music, perhaps even something of politics and political economy. They will know something of "society" as we use the term, and will both seek it and make it. The old home-life will become unbearable to the woman and she will demand the right of choosing her husband just as much as he chooses her. Then the rest will be easy, with its possibilities of inconceivable heights and unspeakable depths.

The great question before the Japanese woman at present is the question of dress. Shall she give up her beautiful and beloved costume, and adopt the strange and uncomfortable attire of the foreign woman, or shall she not? It is a very serious question indeed for her and for her country, and no wonder, as a Japanese friend has just written to me, that "the ladies, who are not accustomed to decision, cannot but feel great pain in their bosom how to make best." The arguments are very conflicting. On the one hand, there is the Empress's own example and her order that no lady shall appear at Court in other than foreign dress. Then there is the natural desire not to appear old-fashioned before their fellows. The desire of their husbands is also in many cases on the side of foreign dress, and so are the public appeals of many influential men, such as the Minister of Education. However, there are certain undoubted advantages of foreign dress over Japanese, such as greater freedom of movement and greater ease and modesty in sitting upon chairs. But on the other side, Japanese women have infinitely too much taste not to see that their own dress is far more beautiful. They know, too, that it is much less expensive, because it is so much more durable and never goes out of fashion. It is likewise evident to most of them that generations of training will be needed before Japanese women can wear the artificial foreign dress as cleverly and elegantly as European and American ladies. Then, too, the public appeal to the women of Japan, signed by Mrs. Cleveland, Mrs. Garfield, and a score of the leading ladies of the United States, trusting that they are "too patriotic to endanger the health of a nation, and to abandon what is beautiful and suitable in their national costume, and to waste money on foreign fashions," has naturally made a great impression upon them.

My friend Dr. Seiken Takenaka, of the Tōkyō Military Hospital, has been investigating this great question, and with German-like precision he has embodied his results in a table. Copies of this table he has caused to be circulated with a popular ladies' magazine, with a request that the fair readers, if they disagree with him on any point, will correct it and return it to him. Thus he hopes to establish a valuable consensus. He compares Japanese and foreign dress for both men and women from the five points of view of hygiene, art, expense, durability, and flexibility—*i.e.*, power of altering a garment so that a mother's will serve for a daughter, a brother's for a sister, a man's for a woman, &c., and his opinions upon this complicated problem are shown as follows :—

	MIDDLE AND UPPER-CLASS DRESS.	MALE.		FEMALE.	
		Jap.	Foreign.	Jap.	Foreign.
HYGIENE.	*a*. Does it deform the natural human body?	no	no	no	yes
	b. Easy or difficult of adaptation to heat and cold?	easy	diff.	easy	diff.
	c. Easy or difficult defence from wind and rain?	diff.	easy	diff.	diff.
	d. Is exercise easy or difficult in it?	diff.	easy	diff.	easy
	e. In summer it is――	cool	hot	cool	hot
	f. In winter it is――	warm	cold	warm	cold
	g. Is the wearer liable to take cold?	no	yes	no	yes
ART.	—As regards beauty (when worn by Japanese) it is――	good	bad	best	middling
COST.	Making	little	very much	little	very much
	Material	— equal —		cheap	dear
DURABILITY		? short	? long	? short	? long
FLEXIBILITY.	—Is it easy to alter?	easy	diff.	easy	diff.
	Result	—	good	good	—

All these decisions seem to me indisputable, except those regarding durability. I should say that both Japanese male and female dress is far superior to foreign in point of durability, and the other Japanese whom I have consulted bear me out in this view. The deductions as to the best dress, Dr. Takenaka draws from his own table as follows :—

Business dress { Male .... Foreign.
                { Female .... Japanese.
Leisure dress { Male .... Japanese.
                { Female .... Japanese.
Night dress .... Japanese.
Invalids' dress .... Japanese.
Children's dress { Boys .... Foreign.
                  { Girls .... Japanese.
Babies' dress .... Japanese.

That is, taking all points into consideration, Japanese dress is best except for boy's clothing and the business dress of men. "Let us reform Japanese dress," he adds, "so as to remedy its defects, taking care not to deprive it of its natural beauty, then we may be sure that we have the best dress in the world." I do not see how anybody who has given attention to the subject can disagree with this conclusion. The question is, how shall the defects be remedied?

The original Japanese belle was "a girl with a white face, a long slender throat and neck, a narrow chest, small limbs, and small hands and feet;" but the best description I know of the Japanese woman as she meets the eye to-day is in McClatchie's very clever and amusing verse translations of some Japanese plays, and is as analytically accurate as it is amusing. This is Lady Kokonoyé:—

"Her figure so trim
As the willow tree's bough is as graceful and slim;
Her complexion's as white as is Fuji's hoar peak
'Neath the snows of midwinter—like damask her cheek—
With a dear little nose,
And two eyes black as sloes,
And a pair of ripe lips which, when parted, disclose
Pearly teeth—her fine eyebrows obliquely are set,
(In Japan that's a beauty)—her hair's dark as jet,
And is coiled in thick masses on top of her pate,

In a wonderful *chignon* as big as a plate :—
(There are *eight* styles of *chignon*, just here I may tell
My fair readers, as known to the Japanese *belle*).
Then, to heighten the beauty bestowed on the part
Of kind Nature, she's called in th' assistance of Art,
For rice-powder to render more dazzlingly fair
Her face, hands, neck, and chin—cherry oil for her hair—
Just a *soupçon* of rouge to embellish her lip—
And a host of cosmetics my mem'ry that slip :—
To complete the fair picture of bright loveliness,
Add to all this the charm of her elegant dress :
    Satin, crape, and brocade
    Here contribute their aid
For the long flowing garments in which she's arrayed,
Which hang loose from her shoulders, in fanciful fold,
All embroidered with storks and plum-blossoms in gold;
Next, a broad velvet girdle encircles her waist,
Tied behind in a huge bow—her feet are encased
In small spotless white stockings, which timidly peep
From beneath her red *jupon's* elaborate sweep;
Add a hair-pin of tortoise-shell, dainty to see;
On her brow place a circlet of gilt filigree."

" In all its essentials," it has been truly said, "the female costume of Japan has remained the same, decade after decade: graceful, artistic, comfortable, and wholesome. The women of this country never abbreviated the interval between themselves and savagery by boring holes in their ears to hang baubles there, by loading their fingers with rings, by encasing their breasts in frames of steel and bone, by distorting their feet with high-heeled shoes, by tricking their heads with feathers, and by sticking dead birds over their raiment." The dress of a Japanese woman of the middle or upper classes begins with the *yumoji*, a rectangular piece of stuff wrapped round the loins and reaching to the knee, like the towel of a shampooer. Over this comes a beautiful garment called the *jiban*, a robe like a perfectly simple bath-gown with square sleeves, fitting quite close to the body, and generally made of delicate and pale-coloured silk crape. In winter an additional garment called the *shitagi* goes over this—all the garments of a Japanese woman after the first petticoat are identical in shape and fit into one another like a nest of boxes. In summer over

the *jiban* comes the outer dress, called for either man or woman the *kimono*. This may be made of pretty cotton stuffs or cotton crape for household wear, or of silk crape or silk, or the richest embroidery and brocade for full dress and ceremonial occasions. It is tied at the waist with a long sash of soft silk crape, called the *hoso-obi*, wound round several times. Round the wearer's waist, above this, is worn that most striking feature of Japanese female costume, the *obi*. This is a piece of the thickest silk or brocade about twelve feet long and thirty inches wide, and may cost anywhere from five to five hundred dollars. It is the pride of the Japanese woman, and a magnificent *obi* is the Japanese equivalent for the conventional diamonds which a lover gives to his mistress with us. The tying of an *obi* is a very difficult task, and reveals the taste and cultivation of the wearer almost as much as the throw of the *himation* did in Greece. Indeed, a woman can hardly tie her *obi* properly without assistance. The stuff is folded lengthwise, giving it a breadth of about fifteen inches, then wound very tightly twice round the waist, with the folded edge downwards, thus making a deep and handy pocket in the fold. One end is measured to the left knee and left loose, then the long loose end behind is turned round at a right angle and let fall into an enormous bow, then the bottom of this bow is gathered up into a smaller inner bow, the short loose end is turned back upon the end of this, and a flat elastic silk band, called the *obi-dome*, is stretched over this to hold both ends and both bows in place, brought round to the front and the two ends hooked together in a little gold ornament of some kind. This description is doubtless unintelligible, but the process is difficult enough to follow, to say nothing of describing it. The costume is completed by a pair of *tabi*, white boots with a separate place for the great toe, like Dr. Jaeger's digitated stockings, the sole made of thick woven cotton and the upper part of white silk. Sometimes a chemisette, or *han-yeri*, of delicately worked or embroidered silk is worn under the *kimono* to show a pretty edge round the open neck and to keep the chest warmer as well.

From this analysis—for venturing on it, by the way, " I humbly beg pardon of Heaven and the lady," as Mr. Pepys did when he kissed the cook —the beauty, hygienic value, and comfort of such a costume are obvious. A Japanese lady in the privacy of her boudoir or to go to the bath can remove everything but the *jiban* and *hoso-obi* and still be exquisitely and modestly dressed—in fact, dressed exactly like a Greek woman. Her clothing can be warm enough for the Arctic regions or cool enough for the tropics without the slightest alteration of shape. The vital organs are protected and supported naturally by the massive *obi*, and its great vertical bow satisfies perfectly, as well as most gracefully and naturally, that desire to have something to conceal the natural shape of the back, which is one of the mysteries of the female mind, and which has developed among ourselves the most vulgar and atrocious article of wear ever invented—the "bustle" or "dress-improver." The defects, of course, of Japanese female costume are that freedom of movement of the legs is impeded, and

AFTER THE BATH.

that while it is perfectly modest for squatting or kneeling on mats, the lower limbs are not covered with sufficient certainty when the wearer moves rapidly or sits on chairs and lounges. This latter defect, the lady signatories of the American appeal declared could be "easily remedied by wearing additional underclothing," and they ought to know. But another plan has been very influentially advocated of late, namely, the general adoption by ladies of the national article of dress called *hakama*, a pair of very loose trousers, the legs of which are so wide that the division between them is seldom visible, with a broad stiff waistband—a "divided skirt," in fact. This would be absolutely modest, it would admit of perfect freedom of movement, it would involve no departure from national habit and ideas, since the *hakama* is a part of the full dress of the Japanese gentleman of to-day, and the appearance of it, with the short hussar-like jacket which necessarily replaces the *kimono*, is charming. But, for my own part, I should regard the sacrifice of the *kimono*, with its long graceful Greek folds, to say nothing of the disappearance of the *obi*, as almost equivalent to the destruction of the beauty of the whole costume. And I cannot see why the *kimono* should not be made wide enough to wrap round the lower part of the body so completely as to serve every purpose of a skirt. Or, better still, the *kimono* itself might be made bag-shaped, either from the neck or only below the waist, and put on over the head, like the *diploidion* of the ladies of old Greece, in which a satyr could not detect immodesty, and movement is perfectly easy, and which I saw charmingly worn in public by a young lady at the performances of the *Eumenides* at Cambridge. That would meet every difficulty without altering even the appearance of the present Japanese dress. The details of Greek costume are quite unknown even to the educated Japanese, and I strongly urge them to experiment upon this suggestion.

The real reason, of course, why the authorities have been setting the example and encouraging the adoption of foreign dress for both men and women in Japan, is a political one. They desire to introduce the foreign manner of living, as the natural corollary and support of foreign institutions, and they know that if they can only make foreign dress universal, Japanese houses will inevitably be replaced by foreign houses, for coats and trousers demand chairs and tables, and these again render the soft matted floors impossible, and then the country will be finally and completely Westernized. One of the gross misconceptions that prevails abroad about Japan—I was told it even while crossing the Pacific—is that foreign dress is now generally worn. Nothing could be more ridiculously untrue. In the streets of Tōkyō, a city of over a million inhabitants, there is perhaps one man in foreign dress out of five hundred —I am inclined to think that one in a thousand would be nearer the mark— while in the country you will not find one in ten thousand.

"THE LATEST STYLE."

In the city you perhaps see two or three Japanese ladies in a foreign dress in a week, but in the country you would not see as many in a year. At a fashionable semi-official ball in Tōkyō there was a large number of the leading ladies wearing foreign dress, and a sadder sight I never saw. Most of them would have looked charming in their own clothes, but as it was (with the exception of one *marquise* who would be beautiful in a flour-sack) they were simply appalling—so badly fitted, the foreign colours so tastelessly combined, so awkward, so ill at ease, that if the spectacle had not been really sad and piteous, one could not have repressed one's laughter. "Voyez-vous," remarked a foreign diplomat to whom I was talking, as he turned on his heel and left the room, "le Japon d'aujourdhui, c'est une traduction mal faite!" The epigram is as untrue as it is clever, but the circumstances fairly provoked it. Except the Court, the Army, and the Civil Service, however, foreign dress has yet no hold in Japan, and almost every man, from the millionaire to the Government clerk, hastens to put if off as soon as he gets inside his own door. And foreign dress and foreign houses and foreign food—it is a case of all or none—mean living at a scale of much greater expense than the Japanese people are at present either willing or able to afford. Moreover, of one thing I am quite convinced, namely that if Japanese women generally adopt foreign dress, the stream of foreign visitors will turn aside from Japan. Instead of beauty there will be ashes—instead of a charm that the world cannot surpass there will be the ugliness from which it apparently cannot escape.

IX.

JAPANESE JINKS.

IX.
JAPANESE JINKS.

JAPAN has been well called the Third Kingdom of Merry Dreams. Amusement is universal here, and so far from it being true that "laughter is man's property alone," everybody laughs — excepting the solemn policeman—men, women, and children, even the very dogs have a twinkle in their eyes as they stretch themselves out over the middle of the streets, and seem to smile as the coolies pulling jinrikishas run round them. For a man would no more think of running over a dog's tail, if the dog did not move, than he would think of pinching his grandfather, and I have been almost jerked out of my *jinrikisha* by the sudden twist my men have made round the long tail which some lazy cur had stretched across the street. I saw a schoolboy steal up behind another schoolboy and hit him a tremendous thwack over the head with a heavy roll of paper he was carrying. Did the first one angrily threaten or attempt to " punch his head " ? Not a bit, he turned round and they both laughed heartily. Many a time my heart has been in my mouth as my two coolies have plunged headlong into a crowd intent on some street performance, and it seemed impossible to avoid knocking down men and women and running over little children. But no, the coolies raise a great shout, shove half the people one way and half the other, and as the spokes of the wheel graze their shins and almost take the top-knots off the little people, do they turn and hurl curses after us, as a crowd responds to such treatment anywhere else? Not they, they just burst out laughing. Sometimes, however, this laughter seems superfluous. Suppose, for instance, at a tea-house entertainment you desire

A *Geisha* Dancing.—V.

(*An Instantaneous Photograph.*)

to make one of the large-sized compliments customary in this country to the diamond-eyed little *geisha* who waits on you or plays to you or dances for you. You pull yourself together philologically, and remember that the politest possessive case is an honorific prefix—*O me*, "the honourable eyes"—that's good—then by a happy thought you add the suffix which denotes the nominative—*O me wa*—what is "stars," you ask yourself. O yes, *O me wa hoshi*—you're getting along splendidly, and then by a flash of linguistic genius you get the crooked idiom for "are in the manner of" all right (of course you've mastered the syntax before), *O me wa hoshi no yō ni*—there remains the crowning adjective with which you are, as a French lady I knew used to say, to make your little effect. This, no doubt, you have carefully loaded yourself with beforehand, so assuming your tenderest and sincerest expression you confidently touch it off—*O me wa hoshi no yō ni senkentaru*—"Your eyes are as supremely beautiful as the stars!" The sentiment is perhaps a trifle hackneyed, but then linguistically as well as otherwise "on ne peut donner que ce qu'on a," and she would hardly expect you to translate her a canto of Rossetti or Coventry Pat-

more. So you have every reason to be satisfied, because speaking Japanese is not quite like playing on a musical box—it is more like the crumpled French horn. But what is this? Everybody ex-

plodes simultaneously into one long wholesome peal of laughter, the little darlings hold their sides and hide their faces in their sleeves, and your particular fancy clasps the hand you had extended to her with a fine Mozartian " Reich' mir die Hand, mein Leben " air and intention, for the entirely prosaic and cold-blooded purpose of saving herself from toppling over sideways. You are naturally highly indignant at such an outrage of your tenderest efforts, and for the next

twenty-four hours you speak Japanese in monosyllables and bully your coolies in "pidgin." Decidedly sometimes Japanese laughter is superfluous. Afterwards you discover what provoked it on this occasion. Your Japanese was perfect up to the last word, but then instead of taking an ordinary word for "beautiful," like *kirei* or *utsukushii*, you must take the biggest of all, and so at the end of a sentence of colloquial Japanese you stuck a Chinese literary word of the most high-flown and dithyrambic character, which none of your lady listeners had ever heard in their lives, producing a total effect infinitely more incongruous and absurd than the bricklaying of "Mike with the gold-plated hod" or the serenade of the Bengali Babu who described himself as being "Contiguous to the portals of thy gate." But the soft-eyed ladykin's laughter has no malice in it, and when by and by, the feast over, she takes your hand and leads you gently away to the place where you deposited "the honourable boots," she would give you a kiss if you wished it (and who would not?) except for the fact that the Western kiss is unknown in Japan, and the native kiss is an evolution to be studied, not an evanescence to be snatched.

While I am on the subject of Japanese philology there are two other stories worth telling. The Japanese salutation "Good-morning," is *Ohayo*, pronounced *O-hie-o*. Now when the former American Minister Judge Bingham arrived at Japan and alighted in state at the pier at Yokohama, the crowd greeted him with cries *Ohayo, Ohayo!* "Durned clever people these," remarked the flattered judge; "how the deuce did they know I was from Ohio?" The other story was told me by one of the Tōkyō editors who speaks English very well. "How do you say 'Good-morning' in Japanese, Mr. Fukuchi?" an American lady asked him. "*Ohayo,* Madam," he replied. "Ah," she said, "that is very easy to remember, because it's the name of one of the States of my own country." Next morning he was walking along, and the lady passed him in a *jinrikisha*. "Mr. Fukuchi," she cried, "Illinois, Illinois!" A little Japanese, by the way, is very easily learned, and if you add to a small vocabulary a dozen or so of the multitude of quaint and pointed Japanese proverbs, and carefully acquire the exact pronunciation of these, you can soon secure a reputation for conversational fluency. Moreover, the presence of an interpreter is a nuisance at the investigation of many of the things that a student of men and manners wants to know. But to speak Japanese with ease and accuracy is an extremely rare accomplishment for a foreigner. As for "English as she is spoke" by the Japanese, I could give dozens of examples. A friend, for instance, who is an educated gentleman, with a high legal degree, wrote to me the other day urging me to travel by a certain route, because there "the scene's delight, the cooler clime, the folk's disinterestedness, all combine to make us happy."

And there is one other specimen I have come across, which seems worth preserving. It is a poem on "The Waterfall at Yoro, near Lake Biwa," and exhibits a delicious mixture of linguistic confidence and Japanese poetic style :—

> "The name is well-known by the all,
> The graceful scene from old to now;
> Not only scene but waterfall
> With silver colour, sail-like bow.
>
> It's thundering shakes country round,
> Dash'd in a cloud of water.
> Small silver balls on loftily send
> Heavy mist and ceaseless shower.
>
> It comes far up the mountain to
> Below, a flow of water, then

A river, with the branches two
Running quickly to the ocean.

Oh ! gentle, gentle, very poor boy,
His mind so obey father's sake,
A sweet sake. Thou, spout out by,
How joyful tears on face he take.

Once and once emperor's visit,
Matter was pleasant, and in sure
Emperor's mind joyful was set;
Honourable name to the year."[1]

But to return to our jinks. These may be divided into High Jinks and Low Jinks—the high fever and the low fever of pleasure. The former are those that must be prepared beforehand; the latter require only the stretching out of the hand—or rather of the legs. Of Low Jinks, again, there is this difference, either you may go to them or you may have them brought to you. A Japanese gentleman does not often go to a theatre, nor indeed, if he is specially careful of his own reputation, to a tea-house; a Japanese lady, never. Therefore the people whose business it is to amuse others hold themselves in readiness to respond at all times to a private summons, and a Japanese host provides after-dinner dancers, or story-tellers, or jugglers,

[1] *Japan Mail,* July 14, 1888.

or musicians, just as at home we should order a Punch and Judy, or a conjurer for a children's party, or a De Lara for the "grown-ups.' The Low Jinks, however, that you go in search of, are more attractive and interesting, as well as much more varied and universal, so I shall deal chiefly with them.

As an example, however, of the ingenuity and charm of the finer kind of Japanese entertainment, here is a description—for sufficient reasons, from another pen — of an evening I had the pleasure of spending at the country seat of Mr. Iwasaki, near Tōkyō. "The house, a summer villa, is built in the chastest Japanese style, of milk-white timbers, knotless and spotless, absolutely inornate, yet so pure in aspect and so fairly proportioned that no structure could accord better with its surroundings. Here the guests were received, and here three times their number might have been amply accommodated. But this would not have suited Mr. Iwasaki's princely ideas of hospitality. Hastily as the party had been got up, only four days having separated the time of its conception from that of the arrival of the invitations, it was found possible to erect, on the east side of the lake, a separate pavilion with spacious verandah, vestibule, waiting-rooms, and a theatre for private theatricals attached. Associating this extraordinary feat with the pavilion's absolute freedom from any suspicion of newness or garishness, its charming combination of neutral tints—pearl-white verandah, mellow brown roof, and celadon walls—the brilliant incandescence of electric lamps pendant from its ceiling and the softer glow of coloured lanterns hanging from its eaves, one could well imagine oneself in some land of artistic fairies. By six o'clock, just as the cool of evening was beginning to succeed a veritable July day, the guests had all assembled. The beauties of the park were of course a theme of universal admiration. These things find no such ardent devotees as in Japan. And since in Japan the farce of attempting to describe them verbally is never attempted, let us loyally observe the national reticence. One feature, however, we may be permitted to notice as thoroughly characteristic of Japanese habits of thought. Emerging from the inner park, where not a solitary weed could be seen on the broad *parterres* or in the pine forests, and resting for a moment on a hill where still stands the rock seat used by the ill-fated Taikun, Yanagisawa's pupil and victim, one passes by devious avenues into a space that seems to belong wholly to the outer and rougher world. By the side of a ragged-edged dusty road, running through entanglements of wild wood and creeper-choked bush, stands a little rustic hovel, furnished with all the rude necessaries that a humble wayfarer might seek. Here hangs a bundle of roughly-plaited sandals, there a string of dried fish; on deal stalls lie hard eggs, beans boiled on their stalks, the perennial cup of tea, the rarer bottle of *saké*, and over all presides a hostess clad in cotton and smiles, with that essentially Japanese air of poverty that loves to be cheerful and clean, and the never absent bamboo vase of wild flowers. The illusion is perfect. You feel that you are a penurious traveller; that the dust of the long road clings to your weary feet; that you have earned a right to rest amid this homeliness, humility and thrift. The lordly park and its luxurious adjuncts fade into the region of blessed memories, and you find it perfectly natural to see His Excellency the Minister of Finance biting at a hard-boiled egg and sipping a cup of *saké*, His Excellency the Minister of Communications coming to terms with a string of *eda-mame*, and the leading banker of Japan munching a sugar-coated *sembei*. This is picnicing with a moral. While Dives takes his ease in his inn, Lazarus—you are gracefully but forcibly reminded—toils along amid the burden, the heat, the dust, and the hardship of a world that has no respect for anything but dollars. The suggestion is not obstinately obtrusive. It cannot long survive the renewed presence of the lake with its rich reflection of environing cedars and sloping sward. But it has added to enjoyment of these luxuries a pensive zest that dispels the last feeling of restraint or conventionality. The dinner—how tamely the word sounds!—was absolutely Japanese, the fitting adjunct of perfectly attired and perfectly graceful little Abigails. The stage was only once used; two of Tōkyō's celebrated *danseuses* briefly displayed upon it a little weaving of solemn paces and waving of tiny hands. For the rest, the easy abandon of a Japanese feast, its hospitable silence and its merry talk, were accompanied only by a brilliant display of fireworks, duplicated in the depths of the quiet lake. The party broke up at various hours between ten and twelve. Such an entertainment does not come to a set and sudden end like a military manœuvre or a mechanical movement. It gradually fades into cessation. You feel when you have reached home that the voices of the merry guests and the musical laughter of the *geisha* must still be ringing in reality, as they are in your recollection." [1]

Nine-tenths of the amusements of the Japanese centre round the tea-house or *chaya*. There are hundreds of these in Tōkyō, ranging from the commonest eating-house to the Japanese Delmonico's, and a dozen or so of reputation and fashion patronised by the men about town. Let us place ourselves in the shoes of one of these when he has either finished his dinner at about seven o'clock or proposes to take it abroad. He has his favourite tea-house, we will say the well-known one called for no conceivable reason *Hamanoya*—" the house of the beach "—or *Bairin*—"the plum grove"—in the Shimbashi quarter, half-a-mile from the railway station. It is in a narrow lane, with nothing outside to guide you except a sign on a paper lamp announcing that cooked food may be had within. No sooner do you slide back the outside door and enter than three or four female figures appear in the dim light and welcome you with a chorus

[1] *Japan Mail*, July 28, 1888.

of *Komban-wa*—"Good evening," and *Shibaraku*—"What a long time since you have been here!" if you are an *habitué*. You doff your shoes, mount upon the raised floor, and one of the figures, which turns out upon closer acquaintance to be a buxom little hand-maiden in a cotton gown, lights a paper candle-lamp upon a long bamboo stem, leads you to one of the rooms of the house and places square leather cushions for you. The "honourable mistress" of the house—*Okamisan*—probably appears for a few minutes; you exchange compliments with her, and Cotton Gown (this has become a proper name, to distinguish them from the silk gowns you will see later) reappears with tea, cakes, and the inevitable tobacco brazier. Then she seats herself upon her heels, smiles wisely and prettily upon you and awaits your orders. She knows, of course, that you did not come to a tea-house to enjoy your own company, and the only question is—though this one also she could probably answer for you beforehand—whom will you summon?

Hereby hangs the story of the *geisha*—that most characteristic and curious product of Japanese social life—and it must be told before we can proceed. For parents who wish to make money out of their daughters there is a way less degrading and hopeless than to condemn them to the Yoshiwara—a way which if slightly less profitable to the parents offers an infinitely more independent goal to the child. They can apprentice her to somebody as a singing girl or *geisha* (pronounced *gáy-shah*). The mortgagee—to use the handiest term—pays a small sum, usually from twenty to fifty dollars, takes the girl when she is fourteen or fifteen, has her carefully instructed in the arts of dancing and playing upon the *samisen*, provides her with beautiful clothes, and as soon as she is proficient in dancing, she assumes a poetical name — " Miss Pine," or " Miss Little Snow," or " Miss Spring Flower "— and he lets her out at so much an hour to amuse the guests at a tea-house or a private party, where she adds the functions of waitress. She is virtually at his disposal for a term of years, so far as all her movements are concerned, and the master or mistress takes the lion's share of her earnings. Her *affaires de cœur* are left theoretically in her own hands. While she is still but a child she is called *han-gyoku* (" half-jewel " —the pay of these girls is poetically called their "jewel," and the present they get, a *hanu* or "flower"), or *o-shaku* ("the cup filler"), or simply *maiko* ("dancing child"), and goes out to dance in company with older girls who play for her; by the time she is sixteen or seventeen she is a **full-fledged** *geisha* (literally "artiste") and **re**sponds alone to any summons to dance, to play, to **wait, or** simply to talk and be chaffed and flirted with, and generally to make the leaden hours fly for lazy and tired men or curious scribblers. If she is clever and good-tempered and full of fun—above all, of course, if she is beautiful— she soon acquires a metropolitan reputation, the young bloods of Tōkyō like **to** be chaffed about her, her engagement list is **full** for days beforehand, you can only get a sight of her by a casual **summons** for an hour or **so;** diamonds appear **on** her fingers and pearls in her hair; she grows **high-spirited;** strange opal-like light flashes at **times in her dark eyes, and** then **some day** she **suddenly disappears. You are invited to** a rich Japanese dinner-party — **she is not** there; you inquire of your friends about her—nobody has **seen** her; at last when you have vainly summoned her a dozen times to a tea-house you are told *Mo hikikomi ni narimashta* — "She has retired"—

"She has Retired."

and you know that she has reached the highest goal of every *geisha's* ambition—some man has fallen in love with her so much that he cannot bear her even to play a part in the amusements of other men, and therefore he has "bought her out,"—*dedecorum pretiosus emptor*—that is, he has paid a sufficient sum of money to induce her master to resign all claims upon her, and has taken her away to his own place. Probably he has paid from five hundred to a thousand dollars for the precarious privilege. A case came within my own knowledge in Tōkyō in which a thousand dollars in hard cash was declined with a smile for a girl for whom twenty-five dollars had originally been paid, and who had been earning for her master over a hundred dollars a month for some time. But the bargain concluded and the honeymoon over, has the happy lover any bond upon his mistress? None whatever, except her gratitude and affection. And will that bond hold? Not always, I fear. It must often happen, of course, that the excitement and varied triumphs of a successful *geisha's* career, render the comparatively dull pleasures of home unbearable to her. Often, indeed, this supposed incapacity to reconcile herself to a quiet life is laid to her charge, but in truth it is not unfrequently the man's heart that plays truant first, and it is the man's fickleness she prettily and touchingly veils in the song that she is most likely to sing you to her *samisen*, comparing herself to the *yanagi*, or weeping willow, and which may be roughly rendered—

> "Wave, willow, high and low,
> Back and forth, and to and fro;
> So the *geisha's* heart must go,
> Where'er the breeze of love may blow."

As for the fickle ones, a *geisha* once confided to me that she was about to be made thus independent by a devoted lover, and added—not knowing that I was but a pilgrim of the quill with no abiding habitation where *geisha* is the local name of the universal being whose promises so many ages of experience have not taught men to distrust—" But I shall be back again in a few months, for I'm sure I shall not be able to bear such a dull life, and then you'll send for me again sometimes, won't you?" For to be in demand, of course, is the *geisha's* professional pride. When she returns to her career after such an episode she enters upon business for her own profit and is mistress of her own actions.

Now the question at the tea-house was, whom

shall we send for? and Cotton Gown sits patiently awaiting an answer. There is Miss Tomoye, tall and handsome and mercenary and mendacious; Miss Kōchō, a quaint little person with a funny face and a quick wit, a magnificent *samisen* player; Miss Koyuki—" Little Snow "—a beautiful girl with a sweet face and soft dark eyes (the eyes, by the way, that provoked the philological efforts described above) and a sad history; Miss Mansuke, tiny and solemn and very pretty and an excellent dancer; and finally " Miss Fate "— well named, for she is of the kind that play Fate's tricks with men. Her slenderness causes her to seem taller than she is; when she moves it is like the flowing of water or the waving of leaves; her complexion is like olives; her eyes are as a pool hidden in autumn woods; her hands and feet are such as exist nowhere but in Japan, and in her the winning wiles of a woman are grafted on the artlessness of a child. She, too, has since disappeared. But on this occasion we ape the Turk and tell Cotton Gown to summon them all—*Mina kakete kure*—and she runs away.

At her bidding downstairs a messenger speeds to a very curious neighbourhood—what may be called Geisha Street. It is a long lane, so narrow that the inhabitants could touch hands across it, filled on both sides with tiny little one-storey houses, before each of which hangs a corpulent paper lantern with a name and a few poetical characters upon it, while from within comes ceaseless merry laughter and the twang of the *samisen*. Here the *geisha* live, and every afternoon about four there is a string of them in loose cotton wrappers of gay patterns going to and from the bath-house. Soon afterwards the messengers begin to arrive, like Porsena's, from east and west and south and north, and a little later, in trios—*geisha* and maid and *samisen*-bearer—the little residents clatter away upon their clogs in all directions.

We have waited perhaps ten minutes sipping our tea when there is a flip-flap of bare feet upon the polished stairs, and then—

> "In comes Nick, to play us a trick,
> In guise of a damsel passing fair."

She twines herself round the corner, and at the threshold falls upon her hands and knees and bows her head to the floor in salutation of each of us. No matter how well you may be acquainted

"Miss Fate."

(*A Japanese Photograph.*)

with her, she never omits this humble ceremony. Then she seats herself among us, pulls a little silver and bamboo pipe and brocade pouch from the massive silk *obi* which serves her as corset and *tournure* and pocket, and enjoys a whiff of the straw-coloured tobacco of the country. The rest arrive one by one, and soon the conversation is merry and the jokes fly fast. The *geisha* makes up for lack of education by ready wit, perfect manners, and a multitude of little clevernesses—games with the hands and fingers, games of forfeits, tricks with pieces of paper and bits of string, *jeux de mots*, besides her stock-in-trade of songs sentimental and songs scandalous, and dances solemn and dances comic. It is her business to entertain you, and she generally manages to do it, even though her own heart is often heavy enough. At a tea-house the fun is not often furious, the space is too confined and the neighbours too numerous, but when a dinner is given you at the private house of some rich man, where the *saké* bowl circulates freely and there are large rooms and gardens and arbours and ponds and boats, then the perhaps two score guests and *geisha* all give themselves up to the most boisterous and wholehearted fun—

"—the joy of frolicking, rollicking,
Doings indulged in by one and by all;
All sorts of revelry,
All sorts of devilry,
All play at High Jinks and keep up the ball!"

Japanese dancing as performed by the *geisha* is

A TUNE ON THE MOON-FIDDLE.

chiefly posturing, with especial attention to the management of the fan. We ask our visitors to dance for us, and one of them sends for her *samisen*—a three-stringed banjo with a long neck and small square head, played with an ivory plectrum—and tunes it with much unpleasant twanging. If she sings, her song is unsympathetic to Western ears; the voice is a nasal falsetto, pitched high even for that, and the method of producing it is so incorrect that a prolonged effort sometimes brings tears into the eyes of the performer. The music of the *samisen*, however, though odd and unintelligible at first, grows upon one, and for my own part I enjoy it now. An ordinary *samisen*, another smaller *samisen*, the violin of Japan, played with a bow, and a *koto*—a kind of thirteen-stringed elongated harp in which the bridges are moved up and down to vary the key during the performance of a piece—usually constitute a Japanese orchestra. The dancer interweaves her paces with but slight grace to an eye accustomed to Legnani and Sozo and Pattie; her rapid turn resembles the right-about-face of an orderly rather than the stepless twine of the *coryphée*. The steps are all made upon the flat of the foot, the toes not being used more than in walking. Nor in such dancing as one sees at a tea-house are there any movements of great strength and agility combined with perfect grace, such as constitute so large a part of the art of ballet-dancing with us. Even the modest *saut de chat* is conspicuous by its absence, and still more of course anything like the *arabesque* or the *ronde de jambes*, which would be as impossible in Japanese costume as they would be foreign to the spirit of the Japanese art. Still, in the undulations of the body, the serpentine movements of hands and arms, and above all in their complete pantomimic skill, the Japanese *danseuses* have resources beyond any of the kind I have seen elsewhere. Among strictly professional dancers, too, marvellous agility is constantly exercised, and I took an instantaneous photograph of one of them, a girl in the huge stiff unwieldly trousers of the old-fashioned style of dancing, which shows her a couple of feet off the ground. There is a sort of club-house in Tōkyō called the Koyokan, or "Red Maple-leaf Club," where the Tōkyō Press Association, comprising the leading metropolitan journalists of all shades of politics meets socially once a month, and there on the occasion when I had the honour of being entertained by my fellow-journalists, a number of Kyotō dancers performed after dinner a series of old dances for us, exhibiting besides the characteristic Japanese charm, terpsichorean ability which would be applauded anywhere. But I am here speaking only of the dancing of the *geisha*.

There is another kind of dancing in Japan, which, to my great regret, I failed to see. A poetical composition of the strictest rhetorical model is sung by one performer to the accompaniment of an instrument or a small orchestra and "danced" synchronously by another. Here is a famous specimen of this remarkable union of two arts. It is entitled *Kazashi no Kiku*—"The Chrysanthemum Hair-Ornament"—composed by Takazaki Seifu, danced by Ichikawa Danjuro, the famous actor. Captain Brinkley has kindly translated it for me. As I have not seen the dancing I must leave the fashion of it to my readers' imaginations.

"O charm against old age, flower of the chrysanthemum!
  Thou that deckest the tresses of happy autumn;
  Vainly they bloom and vainly they wither
  The myriad flowers that open at the four seasons;
  Brief is their life and briefer their glory;
  But thou! No dews bleach thy colour, no frosts mar thy fragrance;
  No chill wind can harm thee, O strength in gentleness;
  Harbourer of peerless odour and loveliness,
  Type of the heart that is changeless and honest,
  Well merited love all ages have lavished on thee,
  Chrysanthemum, emblem of our august Emperor!
  Moistened by dews and dried by the sunshine,
  Over thy mountain dell a thousand seasons
  Thou hast seen pass; till years coming and going

Have brought the prosperity of this bright era,
Even in the age of saints without parallel.
Under the folds of the Rising Sun Standard,
Far and wide the people lift faces of happiness,
Bathed by the dews of Imperial benevolence,
Stoutly to guard the Kingly line, unbroken,
That shall last while heaven and earth have existence,
To hold it above the shocks of countless ages—
Such is the work of the true heart and loyal.
Decked in chrysanthemums, deep-tinted, deep-scented,
Blooming with vigour and glowing with activity,
Glad is the eternal autumn of our Sovereign,
And glad are we in it."

The tea-house is closed by law at midnight, and the rule is generally enforced. As the hour approaches, therefore, the party begins to break up. Each *geisha* receives her "flower," that is, one or two dollar notes wrapped in a piece of paper without folding them. Anything that you give, by the way, wrapped in paper, is a present under all circumstances, and no attempt at concealment is made in executing the pretty fiction of the supposed "flower." You pull out your purse, extract the money, say "May I trouble you for a piece of paper," she gives you a piece from the little roll which every Japanese woman carries in the front of her girdle, wrapped around her pocket-book, and put to the most varied uses—and you wrap up your present and lay it on the ground beside her. Then you all make your way downstairs, the ladykins sit round while you put on your boots, and as you stumble into your *jinrikisha* a simultaneous cry of "*Sayonara!*" speeds you homeward. At the end of the month you receive your bill. I once paid one eleven feet long.

It will occur to most people to wonder what is the personal character of these entertainers of others under such easy circumstances. Are they not as frail as they are fair? Many of them are certainly fairly frail, though some are as chaste as snow, and of those who are the mistresses of some man's heart and pocket it can at least be said of them that they possess the virtue of perfect faithfulness. Poor little mortals, doomed to be merry by profession under all the fatigues and bullying and disappointments of their trying life, "let them enjoy their little day" and pass away escorted by the kindly smiles and tender memories they have evoked. Their class is a disappearing one, for when the Japanese man has assimilated Western amusements as well as Western learning and Western law, he will look for his fun elsewhere than at the hands and lips of these pretty purveyors. His own proverb should remind him, however, that there is such a thing as mending the horn and killing the ox.

X.

IN RURAL JAPAN: A RUSH TO A VOLCANO.

X.

IN RURAL JAPAN: A RUSH TO A VOLCANO.

ON the morning of the 16th of July, 1888, the appalling news reached Tōkyō that an enormous volcano had exploded somewhere in the north of Japan, killing and wounding a thousand people. Japan is the earthquake country of the world, but familiarity with cataclysms, as experience has shown, breeds anything but contempt, the moral effect of them being cumulative rather than diminishing, and this news was received with something like consternation, as possibly foreshadowing a general renascence of volcanic activity. Among foreigners details were first learned at the legations, to be confirmed and amplified next morning by the English and vernacular press. The outbreak had occurred in a group of three mountains, in a remote part of the interior, forming part of the great volcanic ridge running north and south through the country, the chief of them being Bandai-san, situated on the shore of Lake Inawashiro, in the province of Iwashiro, in the prefecture or *Ken* of Fukushima, about two hundred miles north of Tōkyō and midway between sea and sea. And fuller information did not show, as is usually the case, that the first vague accounts were greatly exaggerated. On the contrary, it was certain that the eruption had been one of the most stupendous on record and had caused a frightful destruction of life and property. Besides the difficulty of obtaining accurate information, such an event is among the very rarest experiences of life, and a party was hastily formed to visit the scenes of the catastrophe. Japan is the earthquake and volcano country of the world, after the Philippine Islands, and it was of the greatest possible interest to see for oneself what these outbursts actually are. Moreover, opportunities for seeing the conditions of life in far-off rural districts of Japan are rare. So we left at daylight the next morning, and before we came back we had seen things to dwarf the most extravagant visions of a disordered

A Classic Dance.

imagination, the mere memory of which is enough to make the solid earth seem unreal beneath one's feet.

One of the excellent lines of railway in Japan runs from Ueno, on the outskirts of Tōkyō, nearly due north for 224 miles, passing through the province of Fukushima. Nine hours in the narrow-gauge cars, which are midway between the English and American models in their construction, brought us to the little town of Motomiya, which was the limit of the itinerary we had been able to determine upon before leaving Tōkyō. Installed for dinner at a large tea-house, the hotel of a Japanese village, and our "boys" having astonished the inmates by the sight of a foreign repast consisting chiefly of canned meats and champagne (it is absolutely necessary for most foreigners to take all their food with them on an inland trip, especially over such an unbeaten track as this promised to be). we learned that a ride of about thirty miles in jinrikishas over a rather bad road would bring us to the village of Inawashiro, from which Bandai-san could be reached on foot or on horseback. This would have been entirely satisfactory except for the fact that to carry ourselves, our servants, and our provisions, nearly a dozen jinrikishas were required, and there was not one in the place. A halt of half a day was therefore forced upon us while the vehicles were procured from the nearest town. Tea-house life is feudal in its quaintness, but as unexciting as a Quakers' meeting, and Motomiya, with its one wide street and twenty tributary narrow ones, all flanked with shops where nothing is sold except the most inexpensive necessaries of life, offered neither recreation nor adventure. Under such circumstances an Englishman does one thing the world over—he plays whist. Then the six of us slept soldier-like side by side on the floor under three mosquito nets, and at six the next morning our long procession of jinrikishas trundled away towards the mountains.

The coolie rule is fifteen minutes' rest every two hours, and from six to eight our twenty runners jogged steadily on, their bare legs and bare arms moving with an almost unvarying rhythm, encouraging one another with short sharp cries, or passing the word along to warn against a stone or a hole in the road. The men who are pulling the heaviest man always take the lead, and as our railway magnate weighed something under

twenty stone our pace was decidedly moderate
Still, the road was good, the coolies were fresh,
the morning air was cool and bracing, and it was
just eight o'clock as we spurted up a slope and
sharply round a corner to the tea-house in the
village of Iwanimura, rather less than four *ri*
from Motomiya,—say nine miles in two hours.
So far, the country had been flat and uninteresting,
the narrow road stretching monotonously through
a broad extent of verdant paddy-fields, dotted
with men and women bent double among the
heavily manured roots of the rice-plants, knee-
deep in the evil-smelling mud, half-naked but
sexless in their unsavoury and unending toil.
At Iwanimura, however, the scene changed. A
spotless matted floor, two feet from the ground,
covered with an exquisitely thatched roof, from
which great white bunches of *fu* cakes are hanging, and a kettle boiling over a brazier of charcoal;
a long row of empty jinrikishas; half a dozen
Englishmen in white duck suits and big helmets
sitting on the mats with their feet on the road,
passing around the inevitable flask; a group of
happy chattering villagers looking on with delighted curiosity; a score of half-naked brawny
sun-browned coolies sluicing themselves with

water outside and tea inside and literally pitching the hot snow-white rice into their mouths; a pretty girl with bright brown eyes, a wonderfully white skin, and jet-black teeth, the sign of her wifehood, which she shows all the while in an unbroken stream of merry laughter as she kneels beside each in turn with the tiny tea-cup; in a doorway across the street a long-haired boy—no, it is a slender sweet-faced girl in blouse and trousers, timidly wondering and wondering at these sudden visitants from a strange world; high above us a little gabled house perched upon an overhanging rock, half buried in pines—a Norwegian *saeter* transplanted to another hemisphere; far beyond along the road the cloud-marred outlines of our mountain destination a few *sen* in payment and a whole household bowing with forehead to the floor in a chorus of reiterated *Arigato* and *Sayonara*, "Thank you" and "Good bye";—that is Iwanimura, "the village on the rock," as we saw it for a moment. *Mo yoroshii*, cry the coolies, and we are off.

From this point every mile took us uphill and the landscape rapidly became more broken and rugged, until in two hours' time, when we ran into the village of Takatama and repeated the process of rest and refreshment in another tea-house under the shadow of a high green hill, the country resembled the rolling foothills of the Rocky Mountains, except that instead of being bare and brown it was covered to the hill-tops with brilliant verdure. Here we received our first

OUR RUNNERS AT THE WELL.

information of the eruption. A terrible noise, the people said, had reached them, lasting nearly an hour, and they had all deserted the village and fled, expecting to be overwhelmed. But the noise was all, and by and by they returned. At

Takatama we were nearly half way to Inawashiro, and over the best part of the road we had come fifteen miles in three hours and a half of actual travelling. The mountainous character of the country and its resemblance to Norway now became still more strongly marked; in front and behind us a series of striking and picturesque views sprang up; the little hamlets we passed were idyllic in their situation—they might indeed have been placed upon the stage for the setting of a grand opera without altering a stone or a tree, their graceful gables peeping through willows and maples, above which rose the sloping expanse of pines and firs which covered the base of the ascent, while above these again towered the green mountains. Here the peasants were engaged in the culture of silk; hundreds of flat mat-baskets filled with bushels of cocoons lay about the houses, and through every door we caught a glimpse of men and women reeling the silk thread upon primitive wooden spinning-wheels. As we got further from the ordinary roads of travel, too, dress ceased almost entirely to differentiate sex: men and women, boys and girls, alike wore the blouse and tight trousers of rough blue cotton. It would seem, therefore, that civilization emphasizes sex.

Given unceasing and wholly unimaginative labour for both, and the sentimental distinctions between man and woman are obliterated. "Segregation is asexual," remarked our professor, sententiously. Another curious fact that struck me was the apparent great preponderance of boys over girls among the children.

The road had now become very bad and hilly and the coolies laboured along, wiping the profuse perspiration from their faces. We had been riding for some time by the side of a little irrigating stream running fast downhill to the rice-fields. Soon our men stopped at the foot of a broken ascent and pointing upwards told us that there was a short cut for us, while they must go round by the road. The climb was several hundred yards at an angle of forty-five degrees, by the side of a cascade which poured out of a round hole a few yards from the top. When we reached the top we found that this was fed from an irrigating canal four or five miles long, from Lake Inawashiro, excellently built and bridged with stone and provided with admirable modern sluice-gates. That the remote parts of the country should thus contain public works of first-class engineering reflects great credit on the Japanese authorities. Long before our vehicles overtook us, the rain, which is constant among these hills, burst upon us, and in a few minutes we were wet to the skin and our pith helmets were as heavy as the iron pot-hat of a mediæval pikeman. To ride in such a state would have been to woo a too willing rheumatism, so we simply shut our umbrellas and trudged it for five miles more to the next halting-place, the village of Yamagata, on the shore of Lake Inawashiro. We reached the tea-house there, soaked and reeking, with our jinrikishas trailing behind, soon after noon, having covered altogether about twenty-two miles in six hours. In five minutes we had stripped and donned the Japanese *yukata*, or loose dressing-gown, and a very odd-looking party we were as we squatted round in these flowing cotton robes, all too short for long European legs, while our coolies, naked but for a single loin-cloth, roared with good-natured laughter at the colossal proportions of the member of our party with whom the two unlucky ones among them had led the way. There, as we sat at tiffin, the broad lake stretched out before us, completely hemmed in by green hills mirrored deep in its clear water; the dark group around Bandai-san lowered now more distinctly in sight to our right ; and an obliging Japanese official, already on his way back from the scene, drew plan after plan of the catastrophe for us with his pen and little box of water colours as deftly and rapidly as only a Japanese can. At four o'clock we left him with his tea and telescope, and pushed on round the lake, over a road so bad that it was constantly necessary to walk, until at last it degenerated into a mere path among the narrow paddy-fields. A deserted village, Tsubo-oroshi, literally " the place for putting down the pots," showed the remaining effects of panic. The inhabitants had fled, the little shops were closed, the *amado*, or outside rain-doors, were slid in front of all the houses, and the place was silent and forlorn as though a pestilence had descended upon it. In the midst of the next half-deserted village an official from Inawashiro, our destination, was waiting for us, hat in hand. His Excellency Count Ito, President of the Privy Council, had shown me the distinguished courtesy of causing an official letter to be sent to the *Ken-rei* or Governor of the Prefecture, requesting him to afford me any assistance or hospitality. Consequently on reaching Inawashiro at last, at the farther end of the lake, we found that accommodation, not palatial perhaps, as the village is a small and poor one, but much the best to be had, was provided for us at the house of Mr. Matsui Ginzaburo, the rich man of the place, who kept what we should call at home a general provision and crockery store. Our first impulse was toward a bath, and while appreciating to the full our host's very hospitable intentions, I must say that all the forty smells of Cologne compressed into one quintessential abomination, would rank with the perfumes of Araby in comparison with the paralyzing putrefaction which penetrated into his family bath-room from heaven knows where. For my part, after the first deadly experience, during the three days that we spent under his roof, I remained unbathed. But the principal thing was that we had arrived, and that we could lie down side by side to sleep in the black shadow of death-dealing Bandai.

During the night strange and many-legged insects—"as big as a young trout, bedad," said our Irish companion—roamed around our beds, and the morning was marred by the discovery that our coolies had taken advantage of the payment of a small sum in advance to drown their fatigue in *saké* and that they were all drunk but two or three. This meant an extra walk of five miles for us to the base of the mountain by way of preparation for the day's climb. Then the sober ones struck, on learning that I had promised one of them an additional half-dollar if he took great care in carrying my camera. At last, however, we started, coolies, provisions, cameras and all, led by two guides that the local police had kindly procured for us. The village of Inawashiro is situated at the base of the volcano opposite to that on which the violence of the eruption expended itself, and therefore it escaped injury. It was up this uninjured side of the mountain that we proposed to ascend, and for the first five miles our road was smooth and shaded, leading us through pleasant ascents and between cultivated fields. Then we struck off into the short green scrub, and three miles of this, along a narrow track used by the peasants when cutting fodder for their horses, brought us to the beginning of the ascent proper, where we called the first halt and reunited our scattered party, some of whom had found an elevated and not very safe transport on the top of a huge straw pack-saddle on the back of a half-broken country stallion. The climb now became really fatiguing; it was so steep that an alpenstock was almost necessary and occasionally hands had to come to the rescue of feet; the path wound in and out round trees and over torrents and stones; recent rains had made it slippery with mud, and all the while a tropical sun was beating straight down upon our heads. For an hour and a half, too, there were no more signs of a volcano than there are in Kent or the Catskills; then suddenly our leaders stopped short. We looked about us; there was a smell of sulphur in the air; the leaves at our side were coated with impalpable grey ashes; and there within a few steps was a small crater twenty feet wide, a conical hole blown out as though a hundred pound shell had exploded underground. The first burst had of course exhausted the slight volcanic energy at this point and the bottom of the craterkin was entirely closed. Curiously enough, too, the explosion had been in a lateral direction, trees and shrubs having been blown away, and those left half buried in mud, while a fine tree directly overhead was not only uninjured but not even bespattered. It was only a small affair, but it was our first sight of the actual operation of the volcanic forces of nature, the most mysterious and dreadful forces that man knows, and, a thrill ran through us as we stood around the mud hole. Then we resumed our climb, and half a mile more brought us to the midst of the volcanic activity. In every direction were crater-like holes of different sizes; the trees had been twisted off and split and buried and hurled about; five or six inches of sticky grey mud covered everything; we sank ankle-deep in it at every step, and every now and then as we still climbed, one of the party would struggle back as he found himself sinking deeper, and shout a warning to the rest to avoid the dangerous spot. Pools of dark yellow sulphurous water, small lakes, some of them, had been formed wherever the soil was flat enough for water to rest, and of all the bright turf and foliage which had beautified the spot a few days before, not a single blade or square inch of green was left. It would be impossible—so, at least, we thought then—to imagine a completer picture of utter desolation than this grey and stinking wilderness, all the more terrible that the form of landscape was vaguely preserved in it, just as a mutilated corpse is the more horrible because it cannot mask entirely the graciousness of the living body. Silently and laboriously, panting and perspiring, we plod upwards, watching every heavy step. We are in single file, a guide leading, and I am third in the line. Surely we cannot get much higher, for the mountain seems to end abruptly just above us. The guide is on the top, the man behind him struggles up, seeking a place for his feet. Then as he raises his head, his body being half above the edge, he stops short like a man shot, and slowly and in awe-stricken tone the words fall from his lips—"Good God!" Those of us below shout to him to pass on, and in irresistible excitement and curiosity we scramble up anyhow.

We found ourselves standing upon the ragged edge of what was left of the mountain of Bandai-san after two-thirds of it, including of course the summit, had been literally blown away and spread over the face of the country. Or, to employ the terminology of geometry, the original cone of the mountain had been truncated at an acute angle to its axis, and we were standing upon the flattened apex of the resulting cone. It must be borne in mind, of course, that we had of necessity approached the focus of the eruption from behind, the volcanic energy having exerted itself laterally and not vertically. From our very feet a precipitous mud slope falls away for half a mile or more

till it reaches the level; at our right, still below
us, rises a mud wall a mile long, also sloping
down to the level, and behind it is evidently the
crater, for great clouds and gusts of steam are
pouring over it; beneath us on our left is a little
table-land of mud on which a few pools have
formed. But before us, for five miles in a straight
line, and on each side nearly as far, is a sea of
congealed mud, broken up into ripples and waves
and great billows, and bearing upon its bosom,
like monstrous ships becalmed upon the fantastic
ocean of some cyclopean nightmare, a thousand
huge boulders weighing hundreds of tons apiece.
The sunlight is reflected in weird tints from the
pools and lakes; one larger lake is all that is left
of a river buried at a blow; where the mud has
been coated with ashes it is of a dull grey tint,
elsewhere in spots it is a dark red; on one side
of this awful expanse, a couple of miles away from
us—remember always the colossal scale of the
eruption — a stretch of bright green meadows
sparkles in the sun; on the other a dark pine
forest shows how the sea of mud had rolled up to
its foot and actually stopped there almost touching
the trunks of the trees; and straight in front of us,
five miles away, we can just discern an exit into a

long green valley behind which again rose the mountains, range upon range, dark and grand and solemn, till they pierce the cloudless skies.

But the little table-land below us on the left— what was that? We knew, but who shall tell its tale? It marked the site of the medicinal hot springs of Shimo-no-yu, where a hamlet of invalid visitors, forty or more in number, had been taking the waters, and now springs and hamlet and visitors lie buried under twenty feet of mud, and a few foul puddles form their only monument and epitaph. Eight o'clock in the morning of a bright fresh summer's day; the little place busy with the guests taking their first daily bath; comparing notes, no doubt, as invalids do, of their respective progress towards restored health; the awful rumbling of the earthquake; the explosion, followed instantly by the darkness of death as the cloud of ashes fills the air; one scream of utter terror and despair, and ere it dies away the fall of the sea of boiling mud; then everlasting silence. There is no reason for exhuming them, and no human eye will ever look upon them again to learn the details of their agony. We turn away, for it is impossible to watch these puddles flickering in the sun and think of the poor souls beneath and their awful realization of a *dies iræ*—a day of wrath surpassing even theologic horrors.

To find a spot sufficiently free from mud for us to sit down and open the tiffin-basket, we had to descend a few hundred yards. Then we returned to the same spot and climbed cautiously over the edge and down the slope, our object being to reach the top of the mud-wall I have described as being on our right, and from behind which the steam was rising from the crater itself. The mud was in great cakes and boulders, resting upon the great mass of it beneath—exactly, in fact, like a choppy sea suddenly solidified. The walking, therefore, or rather scrambling, was difficult, and the surface of the mud treacherous. By chance when we had descended far enough in a straight line and turned off to the right to climb to the wall of the crater, two of us happened to be in advance of the rest. Slowly and cautiously we approached the edge, testing the masses of mud before us at every step. At last, side by side and on our hands and knees, we looked over. The mud wall upon the edge of which we stood, sank straight down out of sight into the depths of the abyss and actually shelved in underneath us, so that we were suspended over the seething crater upon no support stronger than overhanging mud, neither solid nor tenacious. Needless to say that after a single brief look we beat a gingerly but hasty retreat. And none too soon, for there between us and the rest of the party was a long

AT THE EDGE OF THE PRECIPICE.

crack several inches wide. But that minute's look will never be forgotten by either of us. For a thousand feet the mud precipice rose straight up to our feet; the crater from which it sprang was probably a mile wide; from a dozen half-visible openings the steam was issuing with the noise of a distant waterfall, while the chief orifice of the crater was altogether hidden by the cloud of steam above it; and whenever the vapour was dissipated for a moment we could see the liquid mud at the bottom, apparently still seething in great disturbance and commotion. The colossal scale of it all, the more than Alpine precipice, the ocean of mud, the buried village, the heat, the steam, the noise, the attempt to picture in imagination the scene when the earth has been thus burst and riven and scattered and convulsed, and the solid land had melted and flowed out as the sea,—all these combined to produce an impression of awe and stupefaction which nothing subsequent can ever efface and with which no previous experiences of life afford the slightest comparison.

We were the first foreigners to make thus a rough but fairly complete examination of the scene of the eruption, and when we started for our long walk home later in the afternoon we were in a position to say with some confidence just what had happened. The main facts of the eruption are these: At the point of the manifestation of volcanic activity the mountain range consists of three peaks which are often spoken of together as Bandai-san, but consist properly of Bandai-san, 5,800 feet, a somewhat smaller mountain known as Sho-Bandai-san, and a third one larger again, called Nekomatadake. The eruption had taken place in the smaller central one of the three, and Sho-Bandai-san has disappeared from the face of the earth. The explosion was caused by steam, there was neither fire nor lava of any kind—it was in fact neither more nor less than a colossal boiler-explosion. The whole top and one side of Sho-Bandai-san had been blown into the air in a lateral direction, and the earth of the mountain was converted by the escaping steam at the moment of the explosion into boiling mud, part of which was projected into the air to fall a long distance and then take the form of an overflowing river, and part of which rushed down with inconceivable speed and resistless force and poured over the face of the country to a depth varying from twenty to a hundred and fifty feet. Thirty square miles of country were thus devastated and practically buried by this eruption, a fact which places it, as I said, among the stupendous on record.

Early next morning our coolies, who had spent

all the money advanced to them and therefore relapsed of necessity into a state of sobriety, ran with us several miles to the village of Mine, on the edge of the mud sea, exactly at the opposite end of the volcanic energy to that we had visited the day before. Indeed, so exactly was the boundary of the flow marked, that the first thing we saw on alighting from our jinrikishas was a house unroofed by the hurricane, up to the wall of which the sea had flowed and stopped. The wall was bent but not overthrown, whereas if the momentum had not ceased precisely at that spot, the whole house would have gone down like a piece of paper in the track of an express train. We were now at the edge of the congealed sea whose source we had previously explored, and its solid billows, strewn with the monstrous boulders, stretched out before us as far as we could see. Over them we clambered to a spot a few yards further on, where a force of men were digging around the roof of an imbedded house to secure the bodies of three of their friends whom they knew to be within. Just beyond this lay one of the smaller specimens of the boulders I have described. I asked some of the men to go and stand near while I photographed it, in order to afford an idea of its size, and in a moment a score of them had climbed on it and stood on the top. Yet among the rocks that had been shot down like hailstones there were some ten times as big as this. Of our day's tramp over the mud it is unnecessary to speak in detail. By and by we had reached a height from which we could see several hundred men and women digging hard on the outskirts of a half-destroyed village. At first we thought they were searching for bodies, but afterwards we discovered that they had neither time nor inclination—nor was there indeed any need—for this, and that they were working so hard to save their rice-fields. Without water they would be ruined in a day or two, and the loss of these would mean starvation and ruin to them. The river Nagase, upon which they were dependent for water, had been buried, and they were making a trench to some small lakes newly-formed by the eruption. Later on we learned that several fights had occurred for these miserable water-supplies between the inhabitants of different villages and that each set a guard night and day over its own desperate attempts at irrigation. Could anything be more pathetic than the spectacle of these poor wretches, barely

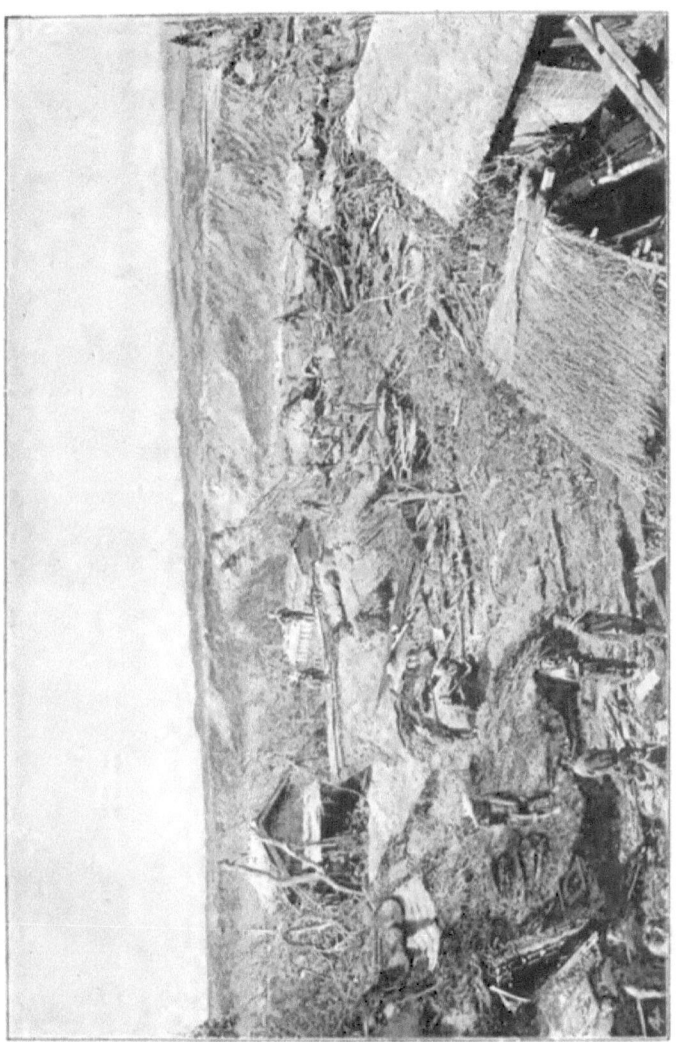

AFTER THE EARTHQUAKE.

escaped from the jaws of a horrible death by being buried alive, taking one another by the throat to save themselves from starvation?

Two hours' steady walking brought us to our goal in the little village of Nagasaka, where occurred the most heartrending scene of all that we can ever know anything of. Ninety lives were lost here, and from three of the half-dozen survivors, by name Watanabe Fusahei, Watanabe Seikichi, and Watanabe Buhachi, I gathered piecemeal the following personal narrative of the catastrophe.

A few minutes past eight o'clock in the morning there was suddenly the most awful noise. Then in a minute, "before a man could run a *cho*" (a *cho* is 120 yards), "darkness darker than midnight, and blinding hot ashes and sand, as you see them here on the roofs," fell upon them. And with the noise came an earthquake so terrible that many of them were thrown to the ground and crawled on all-fours like animals, while the earth undulated like the surface of the sea. Explosion after explosion came in rapid succession, the last one being the greatest, and indeed so great and appalling that after that, they all said, they could not pretend to remember or think what happened or what was the sequence of events. So much is certain, however, that all who could move quickly left their houses instantly and ran for their lives across the village, to ford the shallow stream fifty yards wide and seek refuge on the slope of the hill opposite. Not a single soul of these escaped. And here, to my thinking, is the most appalling fact of all. Bandai-san is 4 *ri* or 10 miles from Nagasaka, as the crow flies. Half of the mountain side which was blown up was shot into the air, and impinged upon the ground a *ri* and a half, or nearly four miles away, and from that point it flowed along in the stream which overwhelmed these people. But the furthest of them was not two hundred yards from the remotest part of the village. Supposing, now, that because of the darkness and confusion and terror it took the swiftest of them, running for his life, five minutes to cover 200 yards—an ample allowance —it follows that the mud-stream must have passed six miles through the air and four miles along the ground in less than five minutes. That is, millions of tons of tenacious boiling mud were hurled over the doomed country at the rate of two miles a minute, or double the speed of the fastest express train! The thought paralyzes one's imagination.

A Fan Dance.

As I have said, of the ninety people who ran, men, women, and children, all perished ; the only survivors were a few old people too infirm to run, and one man, Yabe Sankichi, who had gone over to the hill opposite to cut fodder and was already half way up when the eruption occurred. Watanabe Fusahei, an old man, was in a house with his son aged 32, and his son's child aged six. He begged them to run and save themselves and leave him to his fate : they ran and were engulfed, he stayed and was saved. Many more thrilling stories are told by survivors at other places. One woman was running with her child on her back when a red hot stone flew by and smashed the child. In her terror she did not notice it, however, and ran into a neighbour's house with her red burden upon her back. Another was fleeing and dragging a child by the hand when a boulder struck the child and tore it away, leaving the arm from the shoulder. And the mother was found afterwards alive still clutching the dead hand of her child. But it is useless to repeat such horrors. One man only could have described the whole scene to us, but he had disappeared. This was a peasant who was cutting grass upon a mountain opposite when he heard the noise and saw the ground before him begin to bob up and down. But he had met a fox that morning and now knew that he had been bewitched by it—a common superstition of the Japanese peasant—and that he must above all things keep cool. So he seated himself upon a stone, took out his pipe and watched the whole eruption with perfect equanimity, knowing it to be only a subjective phenomenon! When it was all over, this wily *kitsune-tsuki* — the fox-bewitched — resumed his work, well pleased to have outwitted the evil one. His narrative, if we could have found him, would have been interesting. The aspect of Nagasaka was extraordinary. As the mud stream had passed it by, the houses and their contents, even to the food in the pots, were uninjured, except a few that were flooded by the deflected stream, but there was not a soul to live in them or claim them. A force of police was occupying the village and their red and white flag floated above the roof of the principal house, but it was a delicate task to instal the homeless refugees from other villages there.

Two more sights remained for us, one of pity, one of horror. The police officer who had joined us at Nagasaka led the way across country to a secluded little valley where, in a lonely graveyard under the shadow of the mountains, all the discovered victims lay at last in decent rest. Only twenty-nine there were, in sixteen graves, each an oblong heap of stones from a stream near by, with narrow head-board and monotonous inscription such as, " No. 1. Two men, one woman. Faces unrecognized." From the graveyard the officer led us back to the mud, and a few hundred yards further on our last sight awaited us. As we drew near a crow flew off croaking hoarsely. By the subsidence of the mud another body had been disclosed, and lay at our feet still half imbedded. It was a man, parboiled and of the colour of mahogany, the arms and legs twisted in dreadful convulsions, the skull crushed in, the eyes starting, and the mouth gaping six inches wide, partly no doubt because of death by suffocation and partly by the expansion of the gases of decomposition. That black face, like some fiendish grotesque, haunts me as I write, and it filled our cup of horrors to the brim. We had seen more than enough.

Late that afternoon we started on our homeward journey, to get as far as possible in the cool night air. As we emerged into the path between the rice-fields our runners stopped for a moment, and we all instinctively turned and looked back for a last glimpse of the place where in one dreadful moment a country-side of happy homes and fertile fields and pleasant meadows and green woods had been changed into a grey and blasted wilderness. What we saw was the whole sky behind us flooded by a gorgeous sunset, and old Bandai wreathing himself with a halo of crimson and gold as though he were gloating over his work.

XI.

THE YOSHIWARA: AN UNWRITTEN CHAPTER OF JAPANESE LIFE.

XI.

THE YOSHIWARA: AN UNWRITTEN CHAPTER OF JAPANESE LIFE.

THERE is a place in Japan which every male tourist visits to gaze on its outside; a place that contains probably the most remarkable attempt ever made to solve the great problem of human society; yet a place entirely unknown to the Western world, for nobody has ventured to make in print more than an airy passing allusion to it. No foreigner, indeed, has ever been in a position to write seriously of this place from his own knowledge, for the police authorities tell me that I am the first to whom opportunities for thorough investigation have been afforded. I hesitated of course a good deal before sitting down to write of it, but I long ago concluded not to make one of the conspirators of silence upon all matters of the sexual relations of men and women—themselves not a little responsible for the continuance of the evils they deplore. I have therefore tried to write simply and without impropriety of what I have seen and learned of this remarkable and secret place.[1]

On the furthest north-western outskirts of Tōkyō, an hour's ride in a *jinrikisha* from anywhere, there is a large colony apart. You enter it through a wide gate, on one side of which is a large weeping willow—"The Willow of Welcome" in Japanese—and on the other side a post of police. The streets inside are long and wide, shops and tea-houses alternating; down the

---

[1] I sent a proof of this chapter to the friend whose taste I esteem most highly of all the people I know, with the simple question, "Shall it be included in my book, or not?" This was the reply I received, word for word: "Certainly, it must go in—it can offend no one whose opinion is worth a bootlace. It is clean and simple, and of course it is interesting. Nothing in this world can keep the great problem of sexual relations out of literature to-day and in the future. It must and will go in; everybody will talk and write of it—let us hope, with a great decency—and some fine day a ray of light may strike a bewildered wallowing world."

middle is a beautiful flower-garden, six feet across, where a succession of flowers in full bloom is maintained among pleasant fountains and quaint stone lanterns. An eagle marvellously constructed of shreds of bamboo is sitting upon a tree stump, and half a dozen wax figures of men and women, startlingly life-like, are plucking the flowers and strolling by the fountains. One man has trodden upon a toad and is springing back in disgust, his foot drawn up almost to his waist. A lady has stopped before a little brook and stands with her gown gathered up, hesitating to cross, when a coolie—a Japanese Sir Walter Raleigh—runs up and spreads his coat on the mud before her. These are the wax-works, and all day long a crowd of real people, not a bit more real looking, gaze on them with delight, or with Japanese tenderness and simplicity of feeling find perfect pleasure in admiring the flowers and the butterflies. From the eaves of the bamboo-peaked roof hang two rows of brilliant red lanterns, and from the shops and tea-houses at the side hang two more rows. So in daytime four long lines of red are waving in the wind, and at night four streams of dancing scarlet—appropriate colour!—make the darkness gay. At the end of the principal street is a large and handsome building surmounted by a clock-tower dominating the entire colony. And when you have walked for a quarter of a mile under the lanterns and beside the flowers you find not only one but a dozen such buildings, massive structures of stone and brick with pillared verandas and lofty vaulted entrances through which you get a glimpse of great stairways and columns of polished wood, with cool green gardens extending temptingly beyond. There are no finer buildings in Tōkyō than these, and they have cost hundreds of thousands of dollars. They bear no sign or mark outside to indicate their purpose, though if you look up in passing you will probably see a graceful figure or two in bright gowns strolling upon the balcony, or a pair of black eyes will look curiously down upon you, or perhaps you may catch sight of a graceful head with monumental *coiffure* resting upon a tiny hand and bare arm. This is the Yoshiwara as you may see it any day. What is it, however, if you can look behind the flowers and the lanterns, and read the unwritten story of these silent palaces?

The word "Yoshiwara" means literally "The Plain of Reeds," and so long ago as the reign of the Shogun Iyemitsu in 1659 it was the favourite quarter of the city for the residence of the courtesan class. At the Restoration, however, twenty years ago, the authorities determined to suppress houses of prostitution in the City of Tōkyō proper, and to confine them to this part. Now the word "Yoshiwara" has become the generic name for the quarter inhabited by the Japanese *demi-monde* in any town. There are no fewer than six of them in Tōkyō alone, but the Shin-Yoshiwara, or new one, which I am describing, is the chief and most remarkable. This step of segregation was taken for several reasons. In the first place, it seemed to the authorities that public morals would gain by the removal of the licensed houses, or *kashi-zashiki*, from all the respectable quarters; then the system of regular medical inspection which they were determined to enforce would be easier and more certain; the tax upon each member of the *demi-monde* could be better collected; the whole system, which is regulated by very intricate laws enforced theoretically with great strictness, would be much more under police control; and last but not least in weight, such a quarter would be a happy hunting ground for the secret police, as a successful swindler or a hiding thief would be pretty sure to turn up there, and any conspiracy against law and order would be likely to be discussed there. "Where the carcase is," argued the authorities, "there also will the eagles be gathered together," and the keepers of the *kashi-zashiki* have too much to gain and too much to lose not to help the police secretly by every means—and there must be a million—in their power. So there is a special branch of Yoshiwara Police.

To understand the peculiar Japanese point of view in this matter, we must go back to the Department of Police. There, as I said in my previous chapter, is a special Bureau of Prostitution (included in the Bureau of Trade) with a dozen busy functionaries, and there, too, I was permitted as a special favour to be present at the enrolment of recruits. In a small room on the ground-floor sat two officials behind desks on a raised platform. Opposite them were sliding doors in the wall, and as these were opened from outside by a policeman three persons entered, the girl applying to become a licensed *shogi*, her parent or guardian, and the keeper of a *kashi-zashiki*. They all make very low bows and remain in an attitude of the greatest respect.

The girl is questioned, she replies automatically with downcast eyes; the parent is questioned, he replies apologetically, with many explanations; the keeper is questioned, he replies profusely, with practised fluency. There is a good deal of talk, and the official makes many entries in an elaborately ruled ledger before him. Then the three retire, in a moment the sliding-doors open again to admit another trio, and so on without variation, without emotion, formally and relentlessly the stream of victims is rolled on. I could not help being reminded of the automatic pig-killing at the stock-yards of Chicago. Some of the girls are no longer young, but coarse in person and brazen in manner. Others are delicate and pretty and very frightened. Some look little more than children, bewildered. The parents are quite commonplace people, and the bawds are like their fellows the world over, smug scoundrels. The average number of applications, many of them refused, is about ten daily.

The whole system is based upon the theory of a civil contract. When a girl is forced by her parents or desires of her own will to become a *yujo* or "lady of pleasure," the keeper of a *kashi-*

zashiki is immediately ready to advance to the parents a certain sum of money, say twenty dollars, or fifty, or in very exceptional cases perhaps a hundred. The girl, her parents, and a surety thereupon enter into a bond for her to become an inmate of his house under the ordinary conditions for three years, or until the proportion of her earnings which goes to the keeper (theoretically one-half) is sufficient to recoup him for the sum advanced, together with his outlay for her clothes and board. Should she wish to leave before his complete reimbursement she must refund all the money advanced or expended for her up to that time. If she runs away, the keeper recovers possession of her by a civil action for debt against her parents and surety—a sort of parody of the gruesome action for restitution of conjugal rights, at last, happily, discredited among ourselves. But she can escape altogether by getting beyond her parents' reach and leaving them to settle the debt. When her time has expired, if the refunding process is complete, she is at liberty to leave or to re-engage herself for another term. If it is not complete, she has no choice. And it requires no knowledge of the methods of the trade to

A Processionist of Yoshiwara. (*An Instantaneous Photograph.*)

guess that there will always be a balance of indebtedness on the girl's part. Therefore she stays and stays. She is not allowed to go outside the Yoshiwara without a *kansatsu* or local police pass, and even then she would probably be accompanied by her maid and a male attendant. The examination takes place officially every Monday morning at the police station, the upper floor of which is converted into a sort of surgery (*Kensajo*) for the purpose, and any *shogi* found diseased is immediately conducted by a policeman to a special hospital for such cases. As in England, the ordinary hospitals will not receive them. This hospital is supposed to be supported by the associated keepers, but as a matter of fact they in turn levy a regular tax upon all their *shogi* for the purpose. No girl under 16 is allowed to enter upon the life, and the papers attesting her age must be signed by the officer of the ward in which she resides. All the circumstances of each case, the names of the parents, the reasons why they give their consent, the name of the keeper and the details of the contract, are scrupulously and fully entered in the official ledger of the Department of Police, and the authorities and the law have set up every possible theoretical safeguard between the *yujo* and the keeper, and I believe that these laws are enforced to the letter whenever need arises. But also, it goes without saying that no Solomon could devise theoretical safeguards which would practically protect a girl under such circumstances from unscrupulous greed. For instance, every person in Japan has a private seal corresponding to a signature with us, with which all documents even down to private letters are attested, and to counterfeit or reproduce such a seal is forgery. Now the keeper of every *kashi-zashiki* is compelled by law to keep a big ledger in which all money transactions between himself and the *shogi* are entered, and the *shogi* is compelled to keep a similar smaller book in which the keeper makes identical entries, each of which must be attested by her private seal. This book is regularly inspected by the police with a view to prevent extortion, and it is expressly forbidden by law for the keeper to take away the girl's seal. On one occasion I visited the largest and best *kashi-zashiki* in the Yoshiwara in company with my official interpreter. The keeper was a sharp-looking woman of fifty, who had 45 *shogi* in her house, which she had just built at a cost of 45,000 dollars.

We were taking tea ceremoniously in her private apartments, and after awhile I inquired if I might put a special question to her. "Certainly," she replied. "Any question?" "Certainly." "Then," I said to the old lady through my official interpreter, "will you be so kind as to show me some of the seals belonging to your ladies, that you have at this moment in your possession." She winced visibly and turned several colours, but after a minute got up without a word, trotted off, and returned immediately with the private seal of a certain Miss Man, and I took an impression of it in my notebook, to her evident great alarm. This meant, of course, that she was in the habit of entering the accounts in all the books, attesting them herself with the seals of all her *yujo*, and thus the police would be shown an immaculate record, while the *shogi* themselves would never even see the books, or know with how much they were debited and credited from week to week. It is very unusual, by the way, for one of these great houses to be owned by the keeper; such profitable property is generally owned in Japan as elsewhere by highly respectable capitalists who are never heard of. And profitable indeed it must be, for the market value of land inside the Yoshiwara as compared with the general average in Tōkyō is as four to one. In this Yoshiwara there are 100 *kashi-zashiki* and about 1,850 *shogi*. The Government tax upon each house is 3 dollars a month, and upon each courtesan from half a dollar to 3 dollars a month, according to her class.

There are four classes or grades in the occupation, the renumeration of each being prescribed by law. As everywhere else, the position is polyonomous, *oiran* being the politest name, *shogi* the most frequent, *joro* the most accurate and severe, and *yujo*—"fille de joie"—the prettiest.

THE YUJO.

Each has her own servant and her own apartment, often charmingly decorated with paintings and screens, and adorned with little carvings and porcelain and bits of old silver-work and lacquer, the gifts of various admirers. And there is nearly always a large written and framed scroll in a conspicuous position, exhibiting some scrap of appropriate poetry tersely told in the complicated Chinese characters. One I was shown had the four characters *matsu kiku nao sonsu*, literally, " Pine chrysanthemum still are," *i.e.*, the pine and the chrysanthemum always preserve their charm, even in winter when other flowers die, and by implication, " My charms are everlasting, like the pine and the chrysanthemum."

There are some pleasing beliefs current among foreigners, and which have been circulated in several recent books on Japan, to the effect that it is a common act of filial devotion for a girl to volunteer unasked to devote herself to this life for a term of years in order to pay her parents' debts, to extricate them from some other embarrassment, or even to lay by a little money for herself; and that this done, she returns to the bosom of her family as if nothing had happened, indeed with the added halo of filial piety. This is mostly unmitigated rubbish. "Many girls," says Major Knollys, R.A., for instance, "devote themselves to three or four years' immorality of set purpose, amass comfortable little sums of money, are warmly welcomed back into the domestic circle, and are regarded as models of filial duty in having thus toiled for the support of their parents. In fact, the landmarks between virtue and vice are obliterated." This is a grotesque misstatement. What Major Knollys's sources of information during his few days in Tōkyō may have been, I do not know, but I made searching inquiries on this point in all quarters and from all sorts of people, from the high officers of the Department of Police down to the *yujo* themselves, and I have no hesitation in characterizing the statement as preposterous. It is true that the majority of the girls who enter the Yoshiwara are there that their parents may have money in consequence; but there is not one case in hundreds where they are not unwilling and unhappy victims. The influence of Confucianism has been to implant the duty of filial obedience as the primal and imperative virtue among the lower classes of Japan. A daughter yields absolute unquestioning obedience to her parents under all circumstances. Therefore when they say to her, "You will marry So-and-so," she does not dream of objecting. No more does she when they say to her, "You must enter the Yoshiwara." Of course when she is asked at the Department of Police, "Do you take this step of your own free will?" she replies, "I do," but the case is parallel to the condemned criminal who walks up the steps of the gallows of his own free will.

As for the notion that the life of a courtesan is not considered by the Japanese to involve any particular discredit or disgrace, that is almost equally silly. The reason that such a life here is regarded differently from a similar life in other countries is simply that it *is* different—with just the difference between a person who becomes immoral under compulsion and one who is immoral from choice. The Japanese have their own view of all sexual matters, including this one. *Iroke to kasake no*, they quote philosophically, *nai monowa nai*. And courtesanship among themselves they estimate at precisely its true value. An ineffaceable stain and an irredeemable lowering of personal dignity they know it to be, but they know also that there are not a few cases in which it leaves the moral character untouched. The biography of a famous and beautiful *oiran* named Murasaki says of her, "She defiled her body, but not her heart," and describes her tenderly and prettily as *deichiu no hasu*—"a lotus in the mud." Consequently many an *oiran*, understanding this, looks forward to a respectable marriage with a man whose acquaintance she has made in the Yoshiwara, and a few of them are thus fortunate every year, though perhaps not a larger proportion than in other countries. And as for returning to their families, it is hardly too much to say that they never do. What they think of their own calling may be judged from the fact that when a girl leaves her *kashi-zashiki* to be married or to make any attempt to live differently, nothing would induce her to take with her a scrap of the clothing she has worn there, an article of the furniture of her room, or even one of her knick-knacks from it, although she has paid for them all ten times over. She would regard their presence elsewhere as a constant reproach and shame, so she leaves them for the keeper to sell at ten times their value to the next comer. "When she leaves," I say, but does she often leave? I fear that the female footprints by the "Willow of the Welcome" nearly all point one way. "What are the chief determining causes that recruit the ranks of the *yujo*?" I asked my informants at the Department of Police. "There only two," was the reply; "poverty and natural inclination." "But putting sentiment and theoretical legal safeguards aside, what proportion of *yujo* ever return to a respectable life?" "Unfortunately very few," was the reply; "we have a proverb in Japanese which exactly answers your question, *Ichido doro-midzu ni haittara, isshō mi wo arayenai*—'Once get into dirty water, and you will never be washed clean again as long as you live.'" A few get married; occasionally one commits suicide with her lover because he has not the means wherewith to pay her debts and take her away; an occasional one returns to independence and respectability; but the great majority either die or descend in the scale as they get older and uglier, till they end by being servants in the houses of which they were formerly the ornaments.

It goes without saying that in so strange a community—among these "lotus in the mud"—there is a vast deal of romance, necessarily much more than among the similar classes of countries where vice comes chiefly from choice. Hundreds of novels tell the stories of denizens of the Yoshiwara—of their beauty, their misfortunes, their goodness, their romantic passion and devotion, and their triumph and happiness or despair and suicide. Some of these would be well worth telling if space permitted. As Jesus of Nazareth said long ago, there are often more virtues to be found in the harlot class than in our own highly respectable circle, and I should imagine this to be even truer of Japan than of Jerusalem.

The most extraordinary spectacle of the Yoshiwara takes place for a few afternoons at five o'clock three times a year, when the flowers in the long street gardens are changed. First in spring comes the pink glory of the cherry-blossoms; then in summer the purple of the iris; then in autumn the hundred colours of the chrysanthemum, the national flower of Japan. When the new flowers are planted the *yujo* pay them a state visit. From each of the principal houses half a dozen of the most beautiful are chosen and arrayed in gorgeous clothes, their hair dressed monumentally, combs three feet long stuck in from side

THE VISIT TO THE FLOWERS OF YOSHIWARA. (*An Instantaneous Photograph.*)

to side, and then they are mounted upon black lacquered *geta* or pattens a foot high. When they are ready to start a score of servants accompany them; two or three precede them to put the crowd away; one holds the hand of each *yujo* upon either side, and solemnly and very slowly, a step a minute, the wonderful procession moves round the garden. Other processions issue from the houses and meet and pass, and by and by the whole main street of the Yoshiwara is packed with an open-mouthed crowd, over whose heads the faces of the processionists can be seen here and there.

The walking upon the tall heavy *geta* is itself an accomplishment and girls are specially trained to it. One foot is put out a little way and planted firmly, then the other *geta* is lifted by the toes tightly grasping the strap which passes between the first and second toes, and swung round in front of the other and across it. The first is then lifted and placed on the other side of the second—exactly in fact like a skater doing the outside edge. The Japanese call it *hachimonji ni aruku*—"figure of eight walking." It is difficult to give in words an adequate notion of the extraordinary effect of this procession. The costly and gorgeous clothes of the *yujo*, silks of marvellous richness and brocades blazing with scarlet and gold; the exaggerated bow of her *obi* tied in front (the courtesan is compelled by law to distinguish herself in this way), the pyramidal *coiffure*, the face as white as snow, the eyebrows and eyelashes black, the lips vermilion and even the toe-nails stained pink; the men-servants respectfully holding the tips of her fingers on each side and giving as much heed to every step as an acolyte might give to an aged Pope; her several women-servants walking solemnly behind; a footman pushing back the crowd and another removing every twig or dead leaf from her path; her slow and painful *hachi-monji*; her stony gaze straight before her, half contemptuous and half timid; the dense and silent crowd; the religious aspect of the vicious ceremony,—all these go to make a spectacle apart from anything one has ever seen—an event outside all one's standards of comparison—a reminiscence of phallic ceremonial—a persistence of Priapus.

To complete the picture of the Yoshiwara, I must add that in the lower-class houses the inmates sit at night in the front room on the ground floor, behind wooden bars and plate glass,

HACHIMONJI-NI-ARUKU.

and the passers-by examine them critically at their leisure, like goods in a shop window. Some of them are dressed in what passes for European costume — a sight of indescribable vulgarity and horror. This exhibition is barbarous and offensive in the extreme, and the authorities would be well advised to suppress it immediately.

Such is the great Yoshiwara of Tōkyō. This is not the place to express any opinion upon the principles involved; but as I have written so frankly, it is only fair to the Japanese authorities to point out that their peculiar system has absolutely eradicated the appearance of vice in Tōkyō; you might walk the streets of this city of a million people for a year without seeing a sign of it —a state of things probably without parallel in the civilized world. Then, too, they have dissociated it from riot and drunkenness and robbery; the streets of the Yoshiwara are as quiet and orderly as Mayfair or Fifth Avenue. And nobody in Japan can fall into temptation unwittingly: he must go in search of it. That these are matters of some value at any rate, the people who are responsible for the *police de mœurs* and Mabille, for the Strand and the Haymarket, for the purlieus of Sixth Avenue and the hells of Chicago and San Francisco, are hardly in a position to deny.

XII.
JAPAN FOR THE JAPANESE?

XII.

JAPAN FOR THE JAPANESE?

THERE is one great question in Japan—one question which overshadows for the moment every Japanese art, every phase of Japanese commerce, every Japanese aspiration. There is one point at which Japan touches all the world— one point where Japanese statesmen stand face to face with Salisbury and Harrison and von Caprivi and de Giers and Carnot. The representatives of sixteen nations sat for months round a table discussing it; a long secret memorandum reported upon it to London, to Washington, to Paris, to St. Petersburg, and to Berlin; merchants of every country have eagerly awaited its solution; thoughtful political observers everywhere have watched with alternating approval, amusement, and regret, how the practice of the Great Powers in a typical case has accorded with their familiar professions. I am speaking, of course, of the abolition of the treaties by which Japan is ranked with semi-barbarous races, of the opening of Japan to the enterprise of the world's capitalists, of the admission of Japan to the modern comity of nations.

The first foreigners to break down the Asiatic isolation of old Japan were those most enterprising of early colonists, the Dutch, and for many years before another European foot had trod Japanese soil the Dutch Resident, according to the account of his own physician, had been accustomed on formal occasions to crawl in and out of the presence of the Shogun, and on informal ones "to dance, to jump, to play the drunkard" for the Court's diversion, "with numerous other such apish tricks." In 1854 Commodore Perry, with his great sagacity and his American men-of-war, concluded the first treaty on Japanese soil. Other nations followed suit rapidly. At last in 1858 came Lord Elgin in the *Furious*, fresh from the storming of Canton, the occupation of Tientsin, and the forcing upon China of the epoch-making treaty of that place, and being thus able to fling his sail to a favouring breeze, as the Japanese say, steamed right up to the gates of Tōkyō (it was Yedo in those days) and soon concluded a full treaty upon his own terms, which, to his credit be it said, followed closely the reasonable and generous ones of the treaty which Mr. Townsend Harris, the American diplomatist, had concluded exactly a month before. By this document import duties were reduced from 35 per cent. to about 20 per cent. *ad valorem*, and export duties were fixed at 5 per cent. With one exception, this treaty of Lord Elgin's of 1858 regulates the relations of Japan and the Great Powers at the present moment, for by that insinuating engine of diplomatists, the "most favoured nation" clause, all the European Governments were placed on the same footing as Great Britain. The exception is in this very matter of the tariff. Article XIII. of Mr. Harris's treaty declares the whole of it revisable after the lapse of fourteen years and one year's notice, *upon the desire of either the American or Japanese Governments;* and Regulation VII. adds these plain words: "Five years after the opening of Kanagawa [Kanagawa is practically Yokohama, the former name being still used only in diplomatic and Consular documents], the import and export duties shall be subject to revision *if the Japanese Government desires it.*" In Lord Elgin's Treaty, however, the corresponding passage in Regulation VII. reads, "*if either the British or Japanese Government desires it.*" Thus what Mr. Harris, on the part of the United States, regarded as a just privilege or concession to Japan, in return for what Japan conceded by treaty, Lord Elgin claimed and secured for Great Britain as a right. The enlarged concession soon bore fruit. British cannon had thundered at Kagoshima in 1863 to avenge the murder of Mr. Richardson, and at Shimonoseki in 1865 to open the Inland Sea (a hasty proceeding of which no Englishman can be proud), and the power of the two Japanese clans, at the same time the most powerful and the most bitterly opposed to foreign intercourse, Satsuma and Choshiu, had thus been broken in succession. And during the same period Japan was devastated by the climax of the struggle between the Mikado, the Emperor by right, and the Shogun, the Emperor by usurpation, and the European Powers had at last discovered that making treaties with "His Majesty the Tycoon" was like pouring water over a frog's face, and had insisted that the treaties should be ratified by the rightful sovereign, who was at the time helpless and practically a prisoner, and whose friends had all they could do to keep his head on his shoulders. This was the moment chosen to realize, in the persuasive presence of a large foreign fleet, the opportunities afforded by Lord Elgin's added words; and by the Tariff Convention of 1866, when the Powers had only to ask and have, Great Britain, represented by Sir Harry Parkes, France, the United States, and Holland, knocked off 75 per cent. of the import duties, reducing them to 5 per cent. in theory and a little over 3 per cent. in practice. There is no blame, of course, to be attached to the foreign representatives in this course of action. They had been naturally irritated by delays and incensed by outrages against their fellow-countrymen, and besides, a diplomatist's business is to get as much and give as little as he can, and all moral considerations he leaves where the French general said he left his philanthropy in war time—in his wife's cupboard. But it is only just to the United States to add that Mr. Harris, the man who had opened Japan to foreign commerce, expressed his great regret that the word "revise" had proved in practice to open the door to an enforced continuation of the very relations between Japan and the Western world which he had specially intended it to limit, and declared the conditions to which he perforce agreed to be "against his conscience." And if these were the sentiments of a disinterested foreigner, what must the Japanese themselves have felt and feel?

The conditions of 1858, together with the one made more severe in 1866, are thus, as I have said, the conditions of 1891. They comprise Consular jurisdiction, extra-territorial immunities, the fixing of export and import duties alike at a nominal 5 per cent., the prohibition of the import of opium (one of the few real concessions we have granted to Japanese desire), the opening of five ports to foreign residence and trade, the right to appoint an envoy in the capital and Consuls in the open ports, with similar rights for Japan in the other countries, commercial reciprocity, and the maintenance by Japan (without compensation) of lights and buoys and beacons for the safe navigation of her coasts and harbours.

The outside world has thus stood still for Japan —it has shown her a face as changeless as a statue's—for thirty years. What has Japan done in the meantime? When these treaties were made, her people had not learned to distinguish between Jesuit and layman, and therefore hated them alike, for it is not sufficiently appreciated that the cry of "*Jo-i*,"—"Kill the foreigner" was aimed at the Church of Rome. She was then perhaps the most feudal country history records; two hundred and fifty great nobles, the Daimios, with enormous incomes and two millions of retainers, ruled the land from Ôshiu to Satsuma; when they moved abroad the shout of "*Shita-ni-iro*" — "Bow down" preceded them, and to remain standing was instant death; each of their retainers, fed and clothed by his lord, and ready to give his life in return, had no other occupation than first to study swordsmanship and afterwards to exercise it; he could cut a man's head off by the simple act of drawing his blade from its scabbard; if he struck down a merchant, " He insulted me," was a sufficient excuse and explanation; and any crime that he committed, as well as the least infraction of a code of honour without parallel for punctiliousness, could be expiated by formally disembowelling himself, the *hara-kiri* or *seppuku*, an act for which he was always prepared. Then the Mikado was personally a prisoner, with the functions of a dummy; "since the Middle Ages," said Ôkubo in his historic memorandum, "our

Emperor has lived behind a screen and has never set foot upon the ground. Nothing that has happened outside has ever reached his sacred ears." Then there was a standing prohibition of "the wicked sect, called Christian," and offer of rewards for the denunciation of persons suspected of belonging to it. Then Russians and Dutchmen had been murdered in the streets of Yokohama, the interpreter to the British Legation murdered in Tōkyō, the Legation itself twice attacked, Mr. Richardson murdered, then Major Baldwin and Lieutenant Bird butchered, sleeping British sailors killed in the street at Nagasaki, a body of foreigners fired upon at Hiogo, eleven French sailors shot at Sakai, and the escort of the British Minister himself attacked as he was on his way to visit the Mikado. All of these murders that were premeditated, it must be remembered, were committed from the most patriotic motives by men who were prepared to sacrifice their lives rather than see what they regarded as the desecration of Japan and the outrage of the Mikado. "Could I but tranquillize the Imperial mind," said the testament of one of the last of them, " it would redound to my greatest honour, though I am but a person of the very lowest degree." Then the merchant was only two in the social scale above the man who carried off the bodies of decapitated criminals, and one degree above the common coolie. Then, finally, law was the will of the Daimio, finance was his ability to squeeze the agricultural class, and politics was his intrigue. Such was the Japan of the foreign Treaties.

What, now, is the Japan of to-day? It is late in the day to expatiate upon her marvellous progress. She has at her command an army of 50,000 highly trained and perfectly equipped men in peace and 150,000 in war. Her fleet numbers some of the finest and fastest vessels afloat. Her educational system is an ascending scale from public schools and technical schools and normal schools to a university which has trained men to go out and teach the Chinese engineering at Shanghai, to fill many important well-paid engineering posts on the American railways, to take sole responsibility of several great chemical establishments in Europe, and one of her graduates has been for several years the salaried private experimental assistant of Dr. Hoffman in Berlin, the greatest chemist in the world, a post which hundreds of the best European chemists would gladly fill for nothing but the honour and the opportunity. Her police system is if anything too complete and too well informed, her new Criminal Code has been pronounced by more than one great jurist to be without a superior, and the Civil Code is not likely to fall behind it, while I have nowhere seen or heard of prisons more admirably conducted than the two great ones I visited in Tōkyō, or where the prisoners do such splendid work in such apparent content, amid surroundings which show so little obtrusive authority. What shall one take as a typical test of civilization? No coast in the world is better lighted and buoyed than that of Japan; nowhere are life and property more secure: in no country is universal courtesy so natural and so certain. As for the art of Japan, if that be any test, everybody knows of the exquisite drawings and lacquer and silk and faience and silver and bronze that was produced there before America was discovered. Why, in the very winter that Columbus hoisted his sail, the famous Yoshimasa was inaugurating a new departure with new luxury in the *Cha-no-yu* or tea-drinking ceremony, probably the most elaborate and polished ceremonial that has ever been devised. And the splendid gardens of *Gin-kaku* and *Kin-kaku*—" the pavilions of silver and gold "—at Kyōtō, remain to this day monuments of the same Yoshimasa's taste. But these, although they antedate the New World, are but modern in Japan, for before William the Conqueror crossed the channel and founded at Hastings the England that we know, the Court of Nara was the focus of a marvellous art and a magnificent life which are among the inspirations of Japanese history. And as I have spoken of outrage and murders, there is one more example of modern Japan to show that the book of intolerance has been read aright at last and closed for ever, and that however well it may seem to England and America and France and Germany to show thus to the world that for thirty years they have learned nothing and forgotten nothing, for Japan at any rate the old things are passed away. At Namamugi, on the highway from Yokohama to Tōkyō, beside a well under the pine trees, the spot where Richardson was murdered, stands a monument bearing this inscription :—"In memory of C. D. Richardson, an Englishman, who lost his life at this spot, September 14th, 1862. This monument is erected by the proprietor of the land, Kurokawa Soyo, at whose request the following epitaph was composed by Keiu Nakamura Masanao, December, 1883." I am told that the epitaph itself is a masterpiece of literary construction. It is certainly inspired by a very lofty sentiment, and forcibly presents the lesson of the crime as a noble message of international good-will. The following translation is by Captain Brinkley:—

> "Shed by this sea-shore, the blood of a stranger
> Flowed in a fountain of national progress.
> Strong clans uprising, the hands of the Emperor
> Swayed once again the sceptre of Sovereignty;
> And towards reform the mind of the nation
> Turning, awoke to the rights of the people.
> Who in the homes of the dead or the living
> Knows not this brave man? His name shall be written
> Wherever the pages of history are open.
> I, on this stone his story recording,
> Pray that the thought of the blessings he brought us
> May gladden his heart in the land of the shades."

There are about 2,500 foreigners (excluding Chinese), and over forty millions of Japanese in Japan. For the sake of the former the great Powers of the world have kept the latter in practical bondage since 1858. If it be thought that "bondage" is too strong a term, think for a moment what the state of affairs is. Japan has no power over her own tariff, and is compelled to tax her agricultural class excessively to provide a revenue. She has no jurisdiction over a single foreigner, every one of whom must be tried before his own Consul in accordance with the laws of his own country. Any Japanese with a grievance against a foreigner must take action before that foreigner's Consul, according to that foreigner's law as administered by a man who has frequently had no legal training whatever, for a dozen out of the sixteen Consular Courts are presided over by men whose only education has been in the counting-house. The foreigners in Japan are entirely exempted from taxation, and the treaty limits within which they reside are practically exempt from any law at all, for municipal government is a farce there. Japan has spent five million dollars in lighting and buoying her coasts, and spends 200,000 dollars a year in maintaining the system; but foreign ships pay no light dues, and no harbour or tonnage dues. Yet Japan is absolutely entitled by sacred treaties to change all this.

And what are these Treaty Powers and their interests? The following table [1] tells the story :—

[1] These statistics are for 1887, but the proportions are virtually unaltered to-day.

Countries.	Total Import and Export Trade. Yen.	Number of subjects or citizens residing in Japan.
Great Britain	29,502,053	1,124
United States	24,812,363	475
France	11,841,743	209
Germany	4,932,638	281
Switzerland	745,289	32
Italy	718,750	30
Belgium	346,010	8
Austria-Hungary	315,809	34
Russia	221,233	32
Spain	173,243	3
Denmark	74,375	41
Netherlands	72,326	50
Hawaii	10,655	—
Sweden and Norway	10,086	24
Portugal	1,846	45
Peru	1,184	1
Totals	73,779,603	2,389

These are the sixteen "Treaty Powers," the assent of each and every one of which Japan must get before she can avail herself of the undoubted right to revise her treaties. Fancy Japan's autonomy depending on the consent of Belgium or Denmark or Hawaii or Peru! The notion is ludicrous.

It must not be supposed that Japan has tamely acquiesced for years in this state of things without protests or attempts to change it. The inconveniences and losses and humiliations she has suffered preclude such a supposition. On the contrary, her efforts to escape from her bondage have been dramatic. The curtain rose on the first act in April, 1882, when Count Inouye proposed to the foreign ministers a simple and equitable arrangement according to which Japan should be opened to foreign trade, on the one hand, in exchange for a certain measure of judicial autonomy being granted to her on the other. She stated, namely, that her new Criminal Code was complete and had won the eulogy of the most eminent European jurists, that her Civil Code would shortly be finished, and that she would agree to have every foreigner tried in Japan by a bench upon which properly qualified foreign judges should be in a majority. This proffered arrangement was promptly rejected, the British Minister, I believe, leading the opposition.

In the spring of 1884 a limited measure of judicial autonomy was proposed to Japan—*i.e.*, foreigners were to be partially subject to Japanese law—on condition of a few more " accessible ports " being thrown open to foreign residence and trade. But as was immediately pointed out, first, Japan desired to open the whole country and to have the whole of the judicial control, and until this was done the present foreign ports were more than enough. And for foreigners to be partly under Japanese law and partly under foreign law, would be one degree worse and more confusing, if possible, than for them not to be subject to Japanese law at all. So a long series of desultory mutual communications dragged the question on vainly and aimlessly till the summer of 1886.

Perhaps by this time the best of the foreign Ministers were growing rather ashamed of their attitude towards Japan, but whatever the motive power, the British and German Ministers, Sir Francis Plunkett and Baron Von Holleben, presented to Count Inouye the subsequently famous "Anglo-German Note," proposing to reopen negotiations upon virtually the terms of the Japanese proposal of four years before. The proposal was warmly welcomed, and the sixteen representatives of Treaty Powers met in the Council Chamber of the Foreign Office for week after week and month after month. When the Conference met in 1886 the proposed arrangement contained four articles :—

    1. The whole of Japan to be thrown open to foreign residence and trade.

2. Extra-territoriality or Consular jurisdiction to be abolished.
3. The tariff to be revised.
4. The Japanese codes to be in accordance with the principles of Western jurisprudence, and competent courts established.

When the sixteen ministers and Consuls and the Japanese representative finally got into line in April, 1887, and the proposals were sent forward, the following gigantic conditions had been evolved :—

1. For the criminal portion of a total foreign population of 3,000 souls an array of competent highly-paid foreign judges equal in number to the whole English bench was to be provided. These were to be appointed by Japan, paid by Japan, but dismissible, however, not by Japan, but only by their fellow judges.
2. Japanese and English were to be the official languages of the Court, but any foreign tongue was to be admissible, and therefore a full staff of court interpreters to be provided.
3. The new Civil Code to be "communicated" to the sixteen Treaty Powers eight months

before Treaty Revision comes into operation, and every legal alteration or addition for the subsequent fifteen years to be similarly "communicated."

Such conditions surely need only to be stated to be seen to be preposterous, and the consent of a Japanese statesman to them can only be accounted for by an overwhelming desire to see the fact of helplessness and the stigma of barbarity removed from his country at any price, rather than again indefinitely postponed. No wonder that the American Minister sprang to his feet in the Conference Chamber and exclaimed indignantly, "Gentlemen, we are sitting here legislating for Japan!" For as a representative of one of the Great Powers said to me (I quote his exact words), "It would have been a shame to let Japan put her hand to such an unfair bargain."

In the meantime public opinion in Japan had grown active on the subject of Treaty Revision, and as soon as these conditions were understood it made itself felt in an unmistakable manner. The extra 5 per cent. which Japan was to be allowed to add to her tariff would not more than suffice, it was objected, to pay her foreign judges;

the notion of Japan engaging and paying Imperial servants whom she could not dismiss was characterized as absurd; while for Japan to be compelled to submit all her laws for fifteen years to sixteen foreign countries for approval—including Denmark, Portugal, Hawaii and Peru!—was denounced as a humiliating blow dealt at the national dignity. It was soon evident that no Japanese Government would venture to accept such conditions, and accordingly Count Inouye informed the foreign representatives that Japan would postpone further negotiations until she could lay both her Codes and the composition of her Courts upon the table, when there would be no need of discussing conditions. Soon afterwards Count Inouye resigned the portfolio of Foreign Affairs. Thus everything was "off" once more.

When the storm which forced Count Inouye out of office had subsided, the reins of Foreign Affairs were taken up by Count Okuma. The latter, remembering the failure of trying to treat with sixteen nations at once, adopted the plan of approaching the greater ones separately. The scheme he produced consisted of two points: first, that the revised codes should be printed in

English and promulgated two years before the abolition of Consular jurisdiction; and second, that foreign judges should sit in a majority to try all cases affecting foreigners. If these conditions were accepted he was prepared to open Japan to foreign trade, travel and residence. The United States, Germany, Russia and France at once accepted them. If England had done so too the matter would have been settled. But while England hesitated, Japanese public opinion awoke. The clause about foreign judges was declared to be contrary to the Constitution, and as the time for the assembling of the first Diet (in which for the future power to confirm or repudiate treaties was vested) was close at hand, it was claimed, not without justice, that this momentous question should be postponed for its decision. Again the storm of public feeling broke, and this time it was accompanied by a lightning flash of old Japanese methods. At a Cabinet Council the whole Cabinet decided to resign in a body, and a fanatic lay in wait for Count Okuma at the gate of the Foreign Office as he returned from this council, and threw at him a dynamite bomb, shattering one of his legs, and then, without waiting to see the effect of his blow, cut his own throat and fell dead. It is impossible to describe the popular excitement which ensued, and in the midst of this Count Okuma, who had barely escaped with his life, resigned office. Viscount Aoki succeeded him, and submitted proposals again, but this time shorn of the clause about the foreign judges, which Japanese opinion had finally declared itself against. Since then Viscount Aoki has disappeared from office like his predecessors, the treaties with the United States, Germany, Russia and France have become a dead letter, England has not moved in the matter, but the Criminal, Civil and Commercial Codes, and the Laws of Criminal and Civil Procedure have all been promulgated.

As regards the value of these Codes and the relative position they confer upon Japan, let some one who is qualified speak. Nobody has a better right than the distinguished jurist, M. Boissonade de la Fontarabie, who presided over their creation. Here are his own words: "Le Japon a aujourdhui une Constitution aussi libérale que celle de beaucoup de pays d' Europe. Il jouit depuis longtemps d'une complète liberté religieuse. Les pénalités sont douces et proportionnées, autant et peut-être plus qu'ailleurs, à la gravité des infractions. Les magistrats n'y sont nommés qu'après des justifications d'études sérieuses, et un stage prolongé dans les fonctions inférieures. La magistrature est désormais inamovible. Celle des nations etrangères qui la première donnera aux autres l'exemple de la confiance envers le Japon sera aussi celle qui aura montré le plus de clairvoyance politique et aura le mieux observé le principe fondamental du droit des gens, qui est le respect de l'autonomie des nations indépendantes."

Since the fall of Viscount Aoki Japanese opinion has been daily growing more hostile to concessions of any kind, and more independent. It is the story of the Sibylline books over again. We would not have concessions when they were offered us; they grew steadily smaller at each new offer; now we shall in all probability never have them at all. "At present," said a local newspaper two years ago, "the indignities to which Japan is exposed by the necessity of observing treaties that virtually deprive her of independence are little *en évidence*. Their practical inconvenience is quietly obviated by negotiation, and the general public is not sharply reminded of their existence. But things will be different under representative institutions. Parliament will then become a vehicle for bringing the empire into open and irksome contact with its humiliation. The nation will be publicly reminded that for eighteen years its statesmen failed to assert the independence which was its unquestionable right, and that their thirty years' achievement of enfranchising the people merely meant the mockery of inviting them to legislate subject to the vetoes or approvals of a dozen foreign ministers."

This has now precisely come to pass. Count Okuma was overthrown by a combination of five political parties, whose cry is *Taito-joyaku*—" a treaty on terms of absolute equality." And to-day the most influential party in Japan holds the view that " Japan is the victim of her own weakness, and that her just claims would be at once recognized did she possess the means of enforcing them, or did she make a really resolute effort to have them recognized." Here is a typical expression of Japanese feeling on the subject: "The Japan of to-day is not the Japan of old. The treaties are no longer appropriate. What is wanted is the courage to take decisive action. We must have an army ready to meet any attempt at intimidation, which would in any case not be joined in by all the Powers. If foreigners refuse to listen to us, and resort to unjust measures, we should leave the issue to be settled by war. I hold that in our intercourse with foreigners we should endeavour to cultivate their friendship by observing good faith and justice in our dealings with them. But where our national rights are concerned, where the peace and tranquility of our country are at stake, what we require is energy and courage and to remain firm to the last extremity. Our foreign relations are influenced exclusively by intimidation. There is an old saying that excess of good-nature is akin to weakness; too much courtesy an approach to flattery. Foreigners are guided by selfish policy. Let us abandon the course we have pursued hitherto. Let us increase our military resources, deepen our moats, build formidable fortifications. At the same time let us observe good faith and practice justice while maintaining our dignity. Japan should aim at becoming the leader of Eastern nations, with the aid of twenty powerful men-of-war and 100,000 well-drilled troops."

There is no need for any further argument. The situation is quite clear to any intelligent and unprejudiced observer. All the justice is on the side of Japan, and all the expediency for ourselves, alas. Whether or not England still has it in her power, as she has had for so long, to settle the question by taking the lead, and at the same time to secure for herself the very valuable friendship of Japan against the day when she will stand in great need of it in the Pacific, it is impossible to say. Even if she has, one may well despair of her taking the step. Thirty-one medals were once struck with this inscription, "Presented by the British Government for gallantry in defence of the British Legation, July 6th, 1861," namely, when the Tozenji Temple at Takanawa was attacked by *ronin* of the Mito clan. These were actually presented in July, 1889. During the intervening twenty-eight years they had reposed in a safe in the British Legation! Will British action on the question of Treaty Revision proceed with equal promptitude? *Absit omen.*

I am inclined to think that no foreign government will have much more chance of settling this or any similar question in the future for Japan. At any rate, if I were a Japanese statesman, or the adviser of one, I should say, "denounce" the treaties and announce the expiration of them at a near date. Then let such nations as liked make new ones on terms of equality. Every principle of justice, and two or three of the most powerful nations in the world will be on your side. It is quite certain that no nation will fight for its wretched treaty. And even if it did, there might be worse things for Japan. The gods help those who help themselves.

XIII.

THE FUTURE OF JAPAN.

XIII.

THE FUTURE OF JAPAN.

IN the family of nations (I am sorry I forget who made this clever remark) Japan is the child of the world's old age. And the children of the aged are commonly spoiled. If they are precocious their parents almost always neglect discipline and even justice for the pleasure they derive themselves from their interesting offspring. Now, there never was such precocity as that of Japan. Are we not perhaps spoiling her by our unvarying eulogy?

Such reflections as these must occur to any one who has studied the real Japan of to-day, conceived and frankly expressed the greatest admiration for her, and then after awhile sat himself down to answer the question, "What is to be the end of it all? Is the finished product to be worthy of the aims and efforts that have created it?" The sight of record-breaking is always exciting, but subsequent reflection should prompt the inquiry whether the broken record is worth the struggle and whether the system of the breaker can stand the strain. Certainly no study of contemporary Japan, in which these vital questions are ignored, can claim a respectful hearing. For myself, they recur to me with growing frequency and become more and more difficult to answer confidently as I would wish.

The truth is that in spite of the countless visitors to Japan and the mass of literature about things Japanese, the European world is still curiously far from an adequate understanding of these "Yankees of the Pacific"—ignorant of the common facts of their life and country, still more ignorant of their real character and temperament. An English writer in Japan recently put this very forcibly by a simple analogy: "After centuries of the closest intercourse with our Continental neighbours, how many of the latter have succeeded in describing us so as to escape our derision and indignation. We have been long enough *en évidence* to furnish ample materials for analysis. Our literature is an open book; our domestic habits are well known; our institutions, our social customs, in short, all phases of our public and private lives are, or ought to be, familiar. Yet we are perpetually and grossly misjudged. Is it not reasonable to suppose that Western estimates of Japanese character err at least as flagrantly?" Many of these errors are due directly to blind guides. For instance, to take two or three examples that occur to me at the moment, Miss Bird, plucky and painstaking as she was, fell into an error exquisitely ludicrous but unfortunately indescribable; and Miss Gordon-Cumming made herself responsible for the following nonsense: "In Japan at the present day . . . by law any person inciting another to smoke opium or any person selling it, is liable to be executed. Oh, wise Japan!"[1] Even Mr. Wingfield, cultivated and experienced traveller, delivered himself of the following prophecy a few

[1] "Wanderings in China," vol. ii. p. 306.

years ago : " The Mikado promises at a proximate date a Constitution. It seems more than likely that when the time arrives he and his Constitution will be relegated to limbo, with scant ceremony, as old-fashioned and out of date." [1] It did not need time to refute this forecast : so far as concerns the Emperor it would have been impossible to mistake more completely the Japanese character. Mistakes like these could be collected by the hundred.[2] And indeed, as a local versifier has said—

> "it isn't easy
> For one who's never been to far Japan,
> To know a *kakimono* from a gaily-flowered *kimono*,
> To know a *sayonara* from an *ichiban*."

The common idea of Japanese progress is that a people possessing vast natural charm, courage, intelligence, devotion and health, are being shaped in the mould of a final Western civilization—that consummate experience is being grafted upon primeval virtue. No wonder we anticipate the result with satisfaction. It will be well, however, to divest ourselves for a moment of the effects

---

[1] "Wanderings of a Globe-Trotter," vol. ii, p. 24.
[2] Perhaps the worst offender of all is "A Class-Book of Geography," by C. B. Clarke, F.R.S., Revised Edition. London, 1889.

THE FUTURE OF JAPAN. 341

which the delight of Japan—its natural beauty, the charm of its inhabitants, the fascination of its art—has left upon us, and consider the Japanese people in at least a cool frame of mind, if not actually in a critical one.

To begin with, there is very much in Japanese life that is purely oriental (in the bad sense) and barbaric (in the good sense). I shall never forget my first revelation of this. I was walking in the Japanese town of Yokohama when I suddenly came upon an extraordinary spectacle. Upon an ordinary bullock-cart a raised platform and scaffolding twenty feet high had been constructed, and bullock and all covered with paper decorations and green boughs and artificial flowers. In front a girl with a grotesque mask danced and postured, while half a dozen musicians twanged impossible instruments and kept up an incessant tattoo on drums. Children wild with delight crowded up among the performers and clung like flies all over the cart, and only that providence which takes care of them, together with drunkards and the United States of America, preserved them from making a Juggernaut of it. On foot around the *bashi*, as the whole structure is called, were twenty or thirty men, naked as to their legs, their faces chalked, with straw hats a yard wide, many-coloured tunics in which scarlet predominated, decked out with paper streamers and flowers enough to make a Sioux chief despair of himself, dancing along to a very rude chant and at every step banging upon the ground a long iron bar fitted

A MATSURI IN YOKOHAMA.

with loose rings. The colours, the song, the dance, the music and the clanging iron, formed together a spectacle as barbarous in taste as possible, something wholly different from what one had supposed the gentle culture of the Japanese to be. Yet it was a semi-religious procession—a *matsuri*—corresponding to what one may see in Spain or Mexico or Manila. With the idea of Japan I had brought from Europe I could scarcely believe my eyes: the performance corresponded more to my idea of New Guinea.

A volume could be filled easily with illustrations of this same side of the Japanese character. On the occasion of a beam-rearing ceremony recently at the Hongwanji Temple the ropes were made of human hair contributed by the devotees. There were twenty-four pieces, varying in diameter from four to seven inches, and weighing over 8,847 lbs. It was calculated that 358,883 heads of the faithful were thus despoiled that the temple might be honoured. As a specimen of popular superstition, the Japanese populace believe that a huge catfish lies imprisoned by the weight of the Japanese islands upon him, and that the frequent earthquakes are caused by his ineffectual struggles to free himself. Again, I once saw a crowd of Japanese pilgrims at Nikko eagerly buying charms at a halfpenny each from the temple priests, who were assuring them that the possessor of a charm was secure against an appalling list of possible evils, and safe to enjoy numerous blessings, including a painless delivery in child-birth. To be quite frank, Japan is not infrequently oriental and barbaric even in two of the matters for which she receives in Europe the greatest credit—politeness and cleanliness. Count Goto recently issued instructions to all officials of the Communications Department, of which he was the head, enjoining the duty of treating every member of the public, irrespective of social or official position, with politeness and civility. He would hardly have done this without good cause. And as regards cleanliness, except that of the person, which is preserved by the luxury of the frequent hot bath, Japan is a great sinner. The sanitary arrangements of many even of the best houses are indescribable; those of the middle and lower class houses are often simply unthinkable. The Japanese do not appear to be physically conscious of a foul smell. It is quite common to be offered a room in a tea-house or a bed in an inn, in the close vicinity of something so obvious to the European nose (it would perhaps be more accurate to say the Anglo-Saxon nose) that sickness would be the not distant result of remaining. If the snow-white mats we admire so much in Japanese houses were taken up, in many cases the revelation of dirt beneath would be startling. A paradise of fleas would not be the chief evil. And a correspondent of the *Japan Mail* wrote the other day asking "were there ever such filthy, abominably filthy tramcars as those in Tōkyō?" All this is an unpleasant and ungracious topic, so I will only add that the list could be greatly extended.

There is also in Japan a belief concerning the highest matters of interest, which will strike a European mind as still more extraordinary. When the Emperor [1] has occasion to refer to the origin of his dynasty he is apt to refer to the time ten thousand years ago, "when our divine Ancestors laid the foundations of the earth." When His Majesty promulgated the Constitution he did "humbly and solemnly swear to the Imperial Founder of Our House and to Our other Imperial Ancestors," and did "now reverently make Our prayer to Them and to Our Illustrious Father, and implore the help of Their Sacred

[1] The title "Mikado" is obsolete and inaccurate, and the Japanese dislike the employment of it by foreigners. Educated Japanese, I am told, call their sovereign ."Shujosama," and ordinary folks say "Tenshi-sama," while the expression "Tenno" is used in all official documents. The title "Emperor" is the proper one for use by foreigners.

Spirits." And he further declared that the Imperial Throne of Japan is "everlasting from ages eternal in an unbroken line of succession." The "Illustrious Father" is Jimmu-Tenno, to whom Tensho-Daijin, the sun-goddess, gave a round mirror, her portrait, a sword, a seal and a brocaded banner. A heroic wooden statue of this Jimmu-Tenno, childishly clumsy and inartistic, was awarded the first prize at the great Tōkyō Exhibition last year. Now, there seems a fatal want of harmony between these beliefs, which are devoutly held by every loyal Japanese, and the modern scientific spirit which is supposed to be actuating his country. Between the divine Ancestry of the Emperor on the one hand, and the telephone on the other, there seems an impassable gulf. But since I give this as an example of the oriental and barbaric side of the Japanese character, it is only fair that I should quote the defence of the Emperor's words, which was immediately made by the ablest friend of Japan. "The formula used by the Emperor in the speech from the Throne, was not an invocation of Imperial ghosts. It was simply a stereotyped way of saying that His Majesty does not claim for himself the credit of the things achieved in his reign;

that he attributes them rather to the wise rule of his predecessors, under whose sway the nation has been gradually educated to fitness for the reforms of the Meiji era. The Japanese, indeed, believe that the immortal souls of the dead retain some interest in the sphere where their fondest hopes were once centred and their noblest efforts exercised. They do not suppose that death involves everlasting oblivion to the things and persons among whom life is spent. When the Emperor spoke of the spirits of his ancestors, he undoubtedly expressed his faith that these have always retained and do still retain a benevolent interest in the kingdom they once governed. But what he chiefly sought to convey, what his Japanese hearers chiefly understood by his speech, was that he recognized the work done by previous Emperors, and did not pretend to usurp the credit of progress for which the nation could not have been prepared without their rule. His Majesty will probably be better advised in future. He will hereafter adopt some of the religious formulæ, some of the claims to Heavenly Guardianship, that Western Sovereigns employ when they proceed to cut one another's throats or to steal one another's territories. Having advanced so far in Occidental civilization, Japan must now begin to adopt its cant as well as its culture." [1]

Whether or not this ingenious explanation disposes of the appearance of orientalism and barbarism is a matter for the reader's judgment. The latter may conceivably add, too, that granting the completeness of the superstition, it can be paralleled in Europe. All I desire to express is that these matters I have briefly mentioned, and many similar ones I have not, are as much "the real Japan" as her Codes, her coinage, her cavalry, and her Constitution; and that although many of her statesmen are as enlightened as may be desired, and as I for one know them to be, still they can only work with the material at their command—they can only build their people's progress upon their people's character.

There is another way of examining this question of the future of Japan. Instead of endeavouring to deduce the results from the general character, let us take the results as far as they have been reached at present, and see if the same general character can be inferred from them. The trouble with this method will be that we shall become involved in a mass of apparently

[1] *Japan Weekly Mail*, March 23, 1889.

One Aspect of "The Real Japan." (An instantaneous Photograph.)

contradictory examples. Take the sphere of politics, for instance. The first general election was held last year, when 649 candidates contested 299 seats. The elections passed off as if the Japanese had been electing members of Parliament since the days when the Emperor's ancestors laid the foundations of the earth. "People seemed to regard the affair as a piece of every-day business. There were no crowds, no posters, no bands, no processions, no dead cats, no rotten eggs." But one successful candidate was promptly assassinated in the provinces. One very popular gentleman and scholar in Tōkyō inserted advertisements in the papers asking electors not to vote for him. There was a good deal of corruption, and many candidates were returned without much regard to their personal fitness. But on the other hand, we find a Japanese newspaper addressing these singularly wise words to its readers: "We warn electors that those who bribe them to obtain votes will be the first to sell the interests of their constituencies in the House. There are methods of bribery which, though not defined by law, are as surely bribery as the actual payment of coin. Clean legislators cannot be created out of unclean candidates." It is too soon to say what the new Diet will prove to be; its brief existence seems to have been composed equally of good and bad elements—of acts which promise and acts which threaten. Twenty years ago it was a capital offence to present a petition; now the impeachment of ministers is glibly discussed. The most striking political development of the last few years, however, has undoubtedly been the revival of anti-foreign feeling. Foreigners themselves—or, perhaps, more justly, foreign governments—are to blame for this, but it is a fact of the first importance. The feeling uppermost in the mind of every politically-disposed Japanese of to-day toward the Western peoples whose civilization he is supposed to be envying and imitating, is resentment and anger. The old cry of *Jo-i!*—"Expel the barbarian!"—has been raised again; foreigners have been openly insulted in the streets; one minister has been assassinated, and one crippled by a dynamite bomb for this cause; anti-foreign societies, under such names as *Koku-sui Hozon* —"Preservation of the National Excellencies"— have sprung up, and are described as "a wholesome revolt against self-effacement," while the most sober and thoughtful newspapers calmly state that "her political future is a problem the solution of which Japan reserves for herself." After a public meeting of members of the foreign community of Yokohama to protest against the revision of the treaties in the interest of Japan, the local authorities caused the leaders of the meeting to be personally guarded afterwards by Japanese policemen. This proceeding rather suggests offering a defaulting debtor the services of one's own solicitor, but it shows how much the authorities themselves fear an outbreak of anti-foreign feeling. And since this tide of feeling turned, each minister who has tried to conduct the Treaty Revision negotiations has gone down before it. It is now fairly safe to prophesy that unless a change comes over both parties to these negotiations, the Japanese people will "denounce" the treaties and defy the nations which enforced and desire to maintain them. That is, they will practically say, "The lesson we have learned from you is to repudiate you." I repeat, it will be our own fault, but the fact will remain. The bearing of all this upon the future of Japan is obvious.

It is, perhaps, open to inquiry, after all, how far the startling adoption of Western manners, methods, and institutions, upon which the universal admiration of Japan is chiefly based, is the result of intelligent appreciation, and how far it springs from a national quality of versatile imitation. The former is the condition of education, whether of individuals or nations; the latter reaches its highest development in children and monkeys. "The Japanese think to raise themselves in Western estimation by donning tall hats and frock-coats," wrote even their most friendly critic. "They would rise more quickly by dressing their thoughts in European fashion." It goes without saying that there are plenty of educated Japanese who understand the difference perfectly. Here, for example, is an admirable defence made by the *Hochi Shimbun* against the charge of mere imitation as regards the new Constitution: "Any young country recognizing that for a nation of advanced opinions and sentiments a constitutional form of government is the best, cannot choose but borrow models from the older states of Europe. In point of fact, the English constitutional system has furnished a model for the constitutions of all other countries. Therefore a people contemplating the establishment of a Constitution must commence by studying the

English polity, and then decide for itself what to adopt and what to reject. We may go farther and say that any country possessing a Constitution should be regarded as a teacher capable of imparting valuable instruction. We in Japan can derive our materials from England, America, Germany, France, Austria, and Italy. To supply her own deficiencies from the excellencies of others is the prime aim of our country's emergence from old-time isolation. There is no disgrace but rather credit in imitating what we deem superior, and it is our statesmen's duty to evolve a suitable Constitution for Japan by prudent eclecticism." But innumerable small instances from everyday life in Japan must lead the observer to suspect that by whatever motives the few may be actuated, the many imitate for imitation's sake. I recall a couple of ludicrous incidents of this kind. A certain Mr. Kichiemon, a wealthy merchant of Osaka, desired to celebrate the two-hundredth anniversary of the Wakeko copper mine coming into the possession of his family. The plan he finally adopted was to present each of his three hundred employés with a swallow-tail coat! And another gentleman, Mr. Hegozaemon, who had fallen in with the habit of the New

Year's Day call (imitated from the Americans), improved upon it by leaving on his doorstep a large box with a lid, and this notice above it: "To Visitors. I am out, but I wish you a Happy New Year all the same. N.B.—Please drop your New Year's presents into the box." The following notice, which hangs outside a well-known tobacco-shop, may have been copied from the methods of Messrs. Pears, but it has a wise practicality as well: "When we first opened our tobacco store at Tōkyō, our establishment was patronized by Miss Nakakoshi, a celebrated beauty of Inamato-ro, Shin-yoshiwara, and she would only smoke tobacco purchased at our store. Through her patronage our tobacco became widely known, so we call it by the name of Ima Nakakoshi. And we beg to assure the public that it is as fragrant and sweet as the young lady herself. Try it and you will find our words prove true." Having once begun this tempting subject, it is difficult not to drop one's argument and give pages like the above. I will exercise a rigorous self-control, however, and stop with one more. Over a pastry-cook's shop in Tōkyō I saw this announcement: "Cakes and Infections."

In commercial matters the Japanese have

exhibited their imitativeness in the most extraordinary degree. Almost everything they have once bought, from beer to bayonets and from straw hats to heavy ordnance, they have since learned to make for themselves. There is hardly a well-known European trade-mark that you do not find fraudulently imitated in Japan. The history of Japanese national finance is a romantic model of probity and financial genius, yet every European merchant who deals with Japanese merchants tells you that, in matters of business, they are dishonest and untrustworthy. Many of their great commercial enterprises, such as Mr. Iwasaki's coal mines, or the *Nippon Yusen Kaisha*—one of the most prosperous and admirably-managed great steamship lines of the world—are equal in every respect to the best elsewhere. Yet how absurd these same people can be in simple matters of business is shown by the fact that, when Mr. Iwasaki presented the sum of 10,000 *yen* for charitable purposes to celebrate the promulgation of the Constitution, the committee, in whose hands it was placed, distributed it among 36,338 families, giving them 17·27 *sen*, or less than sixpence apiece! The commercial future of Japan, too, is a matter of peculiar uncertainty. Three years ago there were 76,000 cotton-spindles working in Japan, and 117,000 more building. Yet Rein reported officially to the German Government that Japan would be productive of no great commercial fortunes.

The art of Japan has perhaps more than anything else to do with the question of her future, although this is not apparent at first sight. But, as has been truly said, "Japan owes the place she holds in Occidental esteem to her art, and to her art only." This is at first a hard saying, but the more it is considered, the truer it will be seen to be. Now there is no manner of doubt that the history of Japanese art for the last twenty years shows a marked degradation. And, unless some almost miraculous inspiration should arise to arrest this process, there can also be no doubt that each additional step in the direction of Western civilization will mean another step in the degradation of Japanese art. It was the product of the unique conditions of the past; the conditions of the future will be directly inimical to it. Indeed, the Japanese are often jealous of Western praise of their art, and seem even desirous of hastening its natural decay by the quicklime of ridicule and criticism. "In respect of Japanese civilization," says a recent Japanese writer, "the fine arts have been of little value. On the contrary, their influence has been pernicious. When a Japanese painter has to depict a house, he shows you a dilapidated shanty among ragged plum-trees, and bids you believe that a truly cultured taste loves to gaze upon the moon from such a hovel while the rain patters on the crumbling roof. If he has to limn a landscape he will show you a thatched cottage among mountains, thus teaching you that the acme of human happiness is to live, with, perhaps, a solitary companion—the cottage is not big enough for three—in some isolated region, on a frugal diet of water, vegetables, and acorns. From a poetical, from a musical, from an industrial point of view, Japanese art is opposed to the spirit of active enterprise. It inculcates a taste for seclusion, for poverty, and for restfulness. Such an art can only run counter to the progress of civilization, obstruct the growth of industry, and chill the courage of the nation. Before Hideyoshi's day the people of Japan were not so tame and simple in respect of politics and enterprise as they are now. The development of the fine arts after his time has unquestionably retarded the practical education of the people. Remember . . . that the horse is kept to carry loads; that the ox is well fed for dragging heavy carts; that the silk-worm is regaled upon mulberry leaves in order that he may be robbed of his cocoon, and that the white race, desiring to appropriate the rest of the world, admire the art of Japan, and would have the Japanese lead the hermit-like, star-gazing existence prescribed by that art. As for us, we would ungrudgingly exchange all our fine arts for the envied civilization of Europe. . . A foreigner reared among the surroundings of Western civilization is probably so infatuated with our fine arts that he believes them a replica of the Garden of Eden, a manifestation of divine inspiration, the acme of æsthetic conception. So we, on our side, admire the activity and enterprise of the white race, and envy their wholesome and comfortable manner of living." Such sentiments as these bode ill for the future of Japan, and no wonder that they provoked Captain Brinkley to this retort: "It would be an everlasting pity if the chief endowment of her people, their wonderfully artistic instincts and their not less wonderful facility in expressing them, were left unutilized because a party of fanatical radicals deemed it necessary to commit national suicide in order to be re-born into the comity of Occidental Powers." The "everlasting" element in our pity if this thing happened to Japan would lie in its being *aere perennius*—it would have to take the form of a monument and an epitaph, for whatever new country might arise in its stead, there would be no more Japan.

These are some of the considerations which must influence the student of Japan when he considers the question of her future. They are so difficult to appraise accurately, and often so contradictory, that, whatever opinion he may form for himself, he will hardly venture to express it with much confidence for others. All he will be inclined to say is that the future of Japan is uncertain—that it exhibits more uncertainty, I mean, than attaches to the evolution of human affairs in general. And yet, in conclusion, we have not in the foregoing even touched upon the one vital problem conditioning the future of Japan. Let us admit, for the moment, as it may well prove to be the case, that Japan will succeed in sloughing off whatever innate qualities of orientalism and barbarism she may possess; that her hampering superstitions will drop from her one by one; that her politics will evolve into a perfect mechanism for the adequate and sole expression of her people's will, and for the due realization of that will in institution and administration; that she will learn to regard other peoples with dispassionate criticism and appreciation; that she will intelligently adapt and adopt more and more whatever is excellent whenever she may find it, and slavishly and childishly imitate less and less; that her art will again become the natural and delightful outcome of a unique national artistic endowment; that her commerce and manufacture will grow to equal those of European nations; that her social life will come to be organized and inspired by the best examples—let us admit, in a word, that the Japan of the future will exhibit a "civilization" equal to our own, superior to it, if you please. Will she even then be a gainer by the change? That is, will the mass of the Japanese people be healthier and happier?—there is no other question worth considering for a moment. The Japan of the past, "satellite of that great fixed star, her neighbour," with her feudalism and her despotism, her social ladder of *Shi-no-ko-sho*—"soldier, farmer, mechanic, merchant," in which the latter ranked lowest—her picturesque and kindly superstitions, her punctilious code of personal honour —the most exalted in many ways that the world has ever known, her utter regardlessness of human life in comparison with other things she valued more, her art—the product and distributor of joy, her elaborate and refined ceremonials of social intercourse—the Japan of the past was happy. The first Englishman who visited her, on April 19, 1600, old William Adams from Jellingham, wrote: "The people are good of nature, courteous out of measure, and valiant in war." What could any nation desire further to be? Even to-day the remnants of old Japan bewitch the eyes and the tongues of all who go to her—no words can paint the mind of the traveller whom favouring winds carry to her shores so well as the immortal description of the other earthly paradise of old :—

"Whoso has tasted the honey-sweet fruit from the stem of the lotus,
Never once wishes to leave it, and never once seeks to go homeward:
There would he stay, if he could, content with the eaters of lotus,
Plucking and eating the lotus, forgetting that he was returning."[1]

---

[1] Quoted and translated by Sir Edwin Arnold.

When Japan rings with the rattle of machinery; when the railway has become a feature of her scenery; when the boiler-chimney has defaced her choicest spots as the paper-makers have already obliterated the delights of Oji; when the traditions of *yashiki* and *shizoku* alike are all finally engulfed in the barrack-room; when her art reckons its output by the thousand dozen; when the power in the land is shared between the politician and the plutocrat; when the peasant has been exchanged for the "factory hand," the *kimono* for the slop-suit, the tea-house for the music-hall, the *geisha* for the *lion comique*, and the *daimio* for the beer-peer—will Japan then have made a wise bargain, and will she, looking backward, date a happier era from the day we forced our acquaintance upon her at the cannon's mouth? Those who are satisfied with our own state and prospects will answer easily in the affirmative. For my part, I have been too happy in what remains of old Japan, and too unhappy in what is growing out of "civilization," to be prompt with my "Yes."

www.ingramcontent.com/pod-product-compliance
Lightning Source LLC
Chambersburg PA
CBHW020219240426

43672CB00006B/357